D1569358

ULTRATERRESTRIAL
CONTACT

## About the Author

Philip J. Imbrogno has researched UFOs and other paranormal phenomena for more than thirty years and is recognized as an authority in the field. A science educator at the secondary and collegiate levels for twenty-eight years, he has been interviewed by the *New York Times* and *Coast to Coast AM*, has appeared on NBC's *Today Show* and *The Oprah Winfrey Show*, and has been featured in documentaries on the History Channel, A&E, Lifetime, and HBO. Imbrogno worked closely with many top UFO investigators, including Dr. J. Allen Hynek and Budd Hopkins. He can be contacted by email at Bel1313@ yahoo.com.

# ULTRATERRESTRIAL
# CONTACT

A PARANORMAL
INVESTIGATOR'S
EXPLORATIONS
INTO THE HIDDEN
ABDUCTION EPIDEMIC

## PHILIP J. IMBROGNO

Llewellyn Publications
Woodbury, Minnesota

Portions of this book previously appeared in *Contact of the 5th Kind* (Llewellyn, 1997).

First Edition
Second Printing, 2011

Cover design by Kevin R. Brown
Cover images: shadowy figure © iStockphoto.com/Pali Rao;
    blue grey smoke © iStockphoto.com/Floriana Barbu
Editing by Laura Graves
Illustrations on pages 282–286 by Llewellyn art department

Llewellyn is a registered trademark of Llewellyn Worldwide Ltd.

**Library of Congress Cataloging-in-Publication Data**
Imbrogno, Philip J.
   Ultraterrestrial contact : a paranormal investigator's explorations into the hidden abduction epidemic / Philip J. Imbrogno.—1st ed.
      p. cm.
   Includes bibliographical references (p.   ) and index.
   ISBN 978-0-7387-1959-7
   1.  Human-alien encounters.  I. Title.
   BF2050.I47 2010
   001.942—dc22
                                           2010036626

Llewellyn Publications
A Division of Llewellyn Worldwide Ltd.
2143 Wooddale Drive
Woodbury, MN 55125-2989
www.llewellyn.com

Printed in the United States of America

To Rosemary Ellen Guiley:
Your tireless work in paranormal research
always amazes and inspires me.

## Also by Philip J. Imbrogno

*Night Siege: The Hudson Valley UFO Sightings*

*Celtic Mysteries in New England:*
*Windows to Another Dimension in America's Northeast*

*Interdimensional Universe:*
*The New Science of UFOs, Paranormal Phenomena,*
*and Otherdimensional Beings*

*Files from the Edge:*
*A Paranormal Investigator's Explorations into High Strangeness*

*The Vengeful Djinn:*
*Unveiling the Hidden Agenda of Genies*

# CONTENTS

# ILLUSTRATIONS

# PREFACE

It has been more than thirty years since I've began my investigation of the paranormal. What I've found to be the most interesting has been the UFO phenomenon; of all the strange occurrences on our tiny planet, it is the most complex. One of the most bizarre aspects of the UFO experience is people who claim they've had contact with beings from another world. There are all levels of contact, ranging from the sighting of an alien being or creature near an object that's on the ground, to people who claim to have psychic communication with entities not only from other worlds, but from a parallel reality. When my research began (sometime in the mid-1970s), I shied away from the majority of these contact cases because they appeared to be more psychological than physical representations of the UFO experience. Like many other pioneers in the field, I spent these early years looking for signs of nuts-and-bolts spaceships—I firmly believed UFOs represented technology from alien civilizations visiting planet Earth. As time went on, I began to realize that the contact phenomenon is also part of the total UFO experience and the cases should not be ignored; it should be taken seriously and investigated no matter how bizarre cases may seem. In 1986, I began a study to explore the contact experience in greater detail. At first, only those cases in which the witness claimed UFO-alien contact were considered. Time went on, more data came in my direction, and it became apparent to me that like the UFO experience, the contact phenomenon is extremely complex and not restricted to encounters with physical, extraterrestrial aliens. I decided at that point to expand the parameters of my research and investigate claims of all types involving contact that had taken place with any form of nonhuman intelligence. This category includes extraterrestrial aliens, strange creatures, angels, demons, djinn, and messages from spirits and ghosts. Given the complexity of the phenomenon, it became obvious that the study of UFOs and related paranormal events cannot be restricted to the physical scientist alone. In response to this, I put together a number of research teams over the years that included specialists from many different fields: astronomy, physics, biology, psychology, medicine, engineering, law enforcement, and journalism.

During my many years of investigation, I would often receive calls and letters from psychics claiming to have received a message from extraterrestrials or saying they have "tuned in to" them and could help me predict their next move. At the time, I was very skeptical of these claims and stayed away from working with anyone who said they had psychic abilities. However, one psychic did join my team in the mid-eighties because she proved to possess what I believe to be insight that transcended our normal awareness.

This person has been an integral part of the team ever since. An authentic psychic can play a very important role in investigations of paranormal phenomena, especially when dealing with those who claim alien contact or abduction.

My indoctrination to "big time" UFO research began on March 25, 1983, after an outbreak of hundreds of sightings less than thirty miles from my home. There had been hundreds of reports over the past few days of a giant triangular craft that flew silently over the major highways of New York causing traffic to come to a halt. These sightings are documented in my book *Night Siege: The Hudson Valley UFO Sightings* (St. Paul: Llewellyn, 1995). I will never forget the call I received during that time from Dr. J. Allen Hynek, then the director of the Center for UFO Studies, which at the time was based in Evanston, Illinois. Picking up the phone, I heard a voice I recognized as Dr. Hynek's saying, "What the hell is going on up there?" I updated him about the UFO sightings and shortly after, he came to the area to investigate. Over the next several months, we would spend hundreds of hours in the field investigating UFO reports from credible people who had incredible encounters. Dr. Hynek was so impressed with the quality of the witness accounts that he called the UFO sightings in the Hudson Valley "the most important UFO case in history."

As with any case that involves large numbers of witnesses, there were not only sightings but many people who came forward and claimed some type of contact or communication with an alien intelligence. There were also more than a hundred claims from individuals in that area who said they were abducted by aliens. These cases began to surface shortly after the sightings began, and to me, they seemed an important piece of the puzzle. However, Dr. Hynek didn't want to touch these cases and instructed me not to give them any attention. This decision resulted in several hours of discussion as to what should and should not be investigated in UFO research. Dr. Hynek informed me that he wanted to keep the sightings as credible as possible; he feared that stories of being taken aboard spaceships and meeting aliens might add a circus- or freak-show-like atmosphere to the reports, thus lowering the sightings' plausibility. He said, "You can't talk about [abduction] . . . UFOs are hard enough to believe. We have to have undisputable evidence that can be presented to the scientific community, proving people saw things they couldn't explain in any conventional sense. If you release these reports of alien abductions to the media, they'll have a field day with it." Did Dr. Hynek actually believe that some of these alien abduction-contact cases were real? The answer to that question is yes, he did, but not all of them. As a result of Dr. Hynek's insistence on keeping the matter under wraps, all cases of alien contact (except for one) were kept out of the first edition of *Night Siege*. The one case that did slip in was placed there by me after Dr. Hynek's death in 1986. This was not done out of disrespect—Allen was a close friend, and I admired his work not only in the UFO field, but also in astronomy. It was my intention to inform the readers of *Night Siege* that more was going on in the Hudson Valley of New York than simple over flights of a giant UFO . . . much more.

I realized there was another story to the Hudson Valley mystery—a story so bizarre it would have never been accepted in the 1980s; but today is a different matter. Paranormal events and UFO sightings seem to be on the rise on a global scale and people are more willing to believe that many of the fantastic claims of contact with aliens are possibly true. In 1995, fellow researcher Marianne Horrigan and I released a book named *Contact of the 5th Kind*. This book focused on the material that Dr. Hynek didn't allow in *Night Siege*. This material included sightings of dark triangular UFOs, alien abductions, and contact both on the psychic and physical levels.

After *Contact*'s publication, I realized it didn't tell the complete story, so my research was updated with the addition of new cases and findings which couldn't be released at the time for one reason or another. If you've read *Contact*, you will definitely want to read this book—it takes my research into the twenty-first century, and although several cases presented in *Contact* are also in this book, they are updated. To clarify, this book is not an updated edition of *Contact*, but serves as a new book that details my continuing exploration of the contact experience.

As always, I enjoy hearing from my readers with their suggestions and comments. If you've had an experience involving contact on any level, please write me at the email address given in the "About the Author" section in this book. If you have only a casual interest in the paranormal, are an active researcher, or are just someone who's looking for answers, it's my hope you'll find my work useful in your quest for the truth.

Philip J. Imbrogno
October 2010

# ONE

# SAUCERS VS. TRIANGLES

Flying saucers have been in our modern news since 1947, but for thousands of years, people have reported seeing strange objects in the sky. Although human beings from many diverse cultures have witnessed these objects over the course of human history, reports have been remarkably similar. Interpretations of the UFO phenomenon depend heavily on the period, culture, and personal belief of the witness. For example, in ancient Greece, they were referred to as flying shields and chariots, thought to be the aerial transportation vehicle of some powerful god. In biblical times, they were called clouds, wheels, and angels; in the Middle Ages these objects were thought to be manifestations of the devil and his fallen angels. In 1561, a mass sighting of discs, cylinders, and spheres was seen during the day in the sky over Nuremberg, Germany, frightening thousands of onlookers into thinking the end of the world was nigh. The event was captured in a woodcut and to this day has never been explained.

Strange discs in the sky also appear in religious artwork, usually associated with angels or the Holy Spirit. For example, in Aert de Gelder's *The Baptism of Christ*, painted in 1710, the painting shows what seems to be a flying saucer in the sky projecting down beams of light, illuminating Jesus and John the Baptist.

In the twentieth and twenty-first centuries, we're seeing the same phenomenon as our ancestors. Although they are no longer thought by most to be devils or angels, we call them "flying saucers." In modern times, only in very rare cases are the objects thought to be of supernatural origin. When most cultures around the world think of UFOs today, an extraterrestrial spacecraft containing a crew of alien explorers comes to mind.

## Enter the Flying Saucer

In the mid-twentieth century, the term "flying saucer" was given to a type of unidentified flying object that had a disc-like shape, appearing to be made of silver or another shiny metal. Although these disc-like objects have been reported since the beginning of recorded history, the first highly publicized reports were not made until 1947. The lack of media attention before the twentieth century is strange when you consider that during the eighteenth and nineteenth centuries, people reported seeing what they thought were airships in the sky. The major governments of the world paid no attention to the reports because they were isolated and not very well documented. The first reported sighting in modern times was made on June 25, 1947, by a private pilot named Kenneth Arnold. Although Arnold reported seeing objects that were boomerang-like in shape, he described their movement like "saucers skipping across water"—thus the term "flying saucer" was born. Shortly after his account hit the major newspapers of the world, thousands of people from all over North America reported similar sightings to local and federal authorities. Stories of flying saucers appeared frequently in newspapers, and on radio and television, encouraging people to look up to the sky, mostly out of curiosity, but sometimes out of fear. The majority of the reports from 1947 to 1970 were of silver discs. I find this strange, since the first reported sightings (made by Arnold) were of boomerang-shaped objects. Did the phenomenon take the shape of a disc since it was what the people of Earth expected to see? Reports of disc-like objects continued well into the seventies, but then for some reason, the shape of these unknown objects changed to the black triangle. Before I get into the emergence of the triangular UFOs, let me present several flying saucer/disc reports so the two may be compared.

### The Trent Farm UFO event

The Trent Farm UFO sighting and photograph took place in Oregon on March 11, 1950, and is considered to be one of the best pictures of a flying saucer ever taken. The UFO was seen by a Mr. Paul Trent and his wife at about seven in the evening. Mrs. Trent had gone outside to check on her hutch of rabbits when she saw an object hovering in the sky. She excitedly

*Photograph of disc UFO in daylight by Paul Trent, Oregon, 1950*
*(Photo credit: MUFON [Mutual UFO Network])*

called her husband to come outside with his camera. Paul Trent then came out and took two snapshots of the UFO.

There have been quite a number of attempts to debunk the photograph over the years, and although many skeptics have claimed the photo is a fake, not one of them has ever conducted a detailed analysis of the negative or the original print. The main reason they assume the photo is a hoax is because the image is "too clear." This is a mentality I find very strange because when skeptics look at clear pictures of UFOs, their first impression is that they must be fakes, yet if they look at blurry images, they are more convinced of the authenticity.

I have looked at the Trent photograph a number of times, once using a high power microscope, and noticed what seems to be a thin, straight line extending from the center of the disc, disappearing into the sky. For years, I was convinced this line was some type of wire or string used to dangle a model in front of the camera, giving it the appearance of hovering in the sky at a considerable distance. However, former navy photo analyst and UFO researcher Dr. Bruce Maccabee did an in-depth study of the original negatives and prints and could find no evidence of a hoax. When I questioned Dr. Maccabee about the "string," he informed me that it was most likely a scratch in a multigeneration copy negative—there is no line or "string" in the original.

Today, I'm convinced the sighting and photograph are real because the Trents sounded quite sincere when they gave the press their story. In the weeks following the sighting, the military paid a visit to the Trent home and tried to pressure them into turning over whatever photographs they had. After the visit, Paul Trent was sure that what he photographed was a top-secret military experimental aircraft. The Trents didn't make any money off the UFO photographs; today the images are in the public domain and are available to anyone researching the phenomenon.

### Washington, DC Buzzed by Flying Saucers

Those unfamiliar with the history of the UFO experience often ask the question, "Why do UFOs (flying saucers) only appear in desolate areas?" UFOs are not shy—they have appeared in the skies over some of the most populated areas of the world. In the early eighties, a giant object appeared in the sky over the Hudson River Valley of New York during rush hour, causing bumper-to-bumper traffic. Thirty years earlier, in 1952, a squadron of unknown flying discs buzzed by the Capitol building and the Pentagon in Washington, DC. Evidently, there were two separate sightings over the Capitol: one on July 19/20 at 11:25 PM and the second wave on July 26/27, close to the same time. The sightings were confirmed on ground and air radar, and were seen by multiple witnesses. Although the flying disc sightings certainly caught Washington by surprise, there is little information about the concern it caused in the government. At that time, the military had been studying UFOs for only about four years (since 1948) and although official reports indicated the US government had mixed opinions about the flying saucers as reality, high-ranking members in the army and air force considered the possibility that the unknown objects were real and interplanetary in origin. Despite an attempt to keep the sightings under wraps, the commotion at the nation's capital on both dates convinced many skeptical Americans that these unknown aerial objects were real.

The radar returns received on both sighting dates at Washington National Airport and nearby Andrews Air Force Base were irrefutable evidence of the reality of the discs, creating major concern in all military branches. The objects violated secure American air space with no regard for consequence, and the military realized they had no control over the situation. Blips tracked on radar indicated the objects were traveling at less than 100 mph at first, but then amazingly shot away at almost 700 mph!

As soon as the UFOs appeared on radar, the Air Defense Command scrambled several F-94 fighters to intercept and verify the objects, but by the time the jets arrived at the location, the UFOs had already sped up and vanished. Our jets returned to the ground, and as soon as they did, the UFOs appeared on radar once again. So, once again the jets were sent to investigate, but fortunately, this time they had visual on the objects. As they closed in, all ten targets vanished into thin air.

On July 26, the objects once again appeared on the radar screens at Andrews AFB and the Washington National Airport. As soon as the objects were spotted, several F-94s were deployed to confront the mystery aircraft. As the pilots approached, the UFOs once again vanished. An official report made by the Air Material Command stated that at least one pilot got close enough to see the objects and reported that there were at least ten discs, silver in color, each about thirty feet across. It seems that the flying discs were very interested in the pilot because several of the discs surrounded his aircraft. The pilot radioed his control base, indicated the objects were all around him, and asked for further instructions. He was told to stand down and let the objects continue on their flight path. Under no circumstances was he to engage them. Shortly afterwards, the flying discs moved away at great speed and vanished.

In the days to follow, a number of newspapers, including the *New York Times,* published stories about the sightings. After an exhaustive check into the archives of numerous publications, I found the original *Times* article covering the Washington incident. I was surprised to find a small article, and it was clear that the paper didn't take the flying saucer report seriously; the story was merely filler. It's possible the military told the pilots and the press not to give the incident much publicity so the public would quickly forget. If this was the case, it worked, because in the weeks that followed, the average American citizen forgot about the night the saucers buzzed the capital. The *New York Times* story appears below.[1] I found it interesting that the first sightings took place on July 19/20, yet the story was not published until July 22. To me, the delay indicates the military may have held the story until it had a better handle on what actually took place.

### STRANGE OBJECTS IN THE SKY: FLYING SAUCERS SEEN ON RADAR OVER WASHINGTON, DC

*From: the New York Times Washington Correspondent: Washington, DC, July 22, 1952.*

The Air Force announced last night that the objects had appeared on the radar screen in the air route traffic control centre at the National Airport, first on one section of the screen, and then soon afterwards, on another section, which showed them moving in a different direction. Their speed was only 100 to 135 miles an hour, which is very slow for "flying saucers." One pilot watched the objects for about twelve minutes as he flew from Washington to Martinsburg, West Virginia. Another pilot reported that a brilliant light had followed his aircraft from Herndon, Virginia to within four miles of the National Airport.

On July 29, 1952, the air force held a press conference concerning the sightings because some of the smaller news-

---

1 *New York Times*. "Strange Objects in the Sky: Flying Saucers Seen on Radar Over Washington, DC." July 22, 1952.

papers were playing the incident up with headlines like "Saucers Invade Washington." Major General John Samford informed the media that sightings were caused by weather inversions in the atmosphere and there were no real solid objects in the sky. He also said that ground lights reflected off the clouds giving the impression that lighted disc-like objects were flying overhead. Although most of the American public was satisfied with this explanation, many found it unlikely that our jet pilots were fooled into chasing mirages. The UFOs over Washington, DC, were seen by many witnesses on the ground; some were even able to take photographs. It's important that I mention here that witnesses in DC included people of high status and reputation such as scientists and military personnel.

### The Black Disc

In the autumn of 1978, during an air show in east Hartford, Connecticut, a number of spectators photographing planes from the ground observed a black disc-like object sort of resembling a dirigible in the sky. The UFO emerged from the western horizon and continued east until it was almost directly overhead. People attending at first thought this strange aircraft was part of the program, perhaps some type of experimental aircraft. The object was estimated to be at least ten thousand feet above ground and perhaps the size of a 727. The object didn't make a sound, and the strangest thing of all was that despite being in direct sunlight, the object was jet black. A number of people began taking photographs, but the object accelerated and shot straight up into the air, whereupon

A black disc UFO seen over daylight skies in
west Hartford, Connecticut, 1978 (Photo credit: author)

it vanished. Its departure was noiseless and no sign of engine exhaust was visible.

Afterwards, one of the witnesses contacted me and showed me the photo he had taken. I was surprised at how dark the object looked; when the photograph was blown up to fifty times magnification, it showed an object with notable projections of some sort. My first step in this investigation was to find additional witnesses. Because stories of the sighting appeared in many Connecticut newspapers, I had no trouble finding other witnesses who had seen the object at the air show that day. I spoke with six additional witnesses—all of them told similar stories of how a silent, dark object appeared in the sky and quickly shot almost straight upwards into the sky.

I sent a copy of the photograph to the Federal Aviation Administration who, to my surprise, quickly contacted me to report that no aircraft or blimps were in the area at the time and nothing was spotted on radar at nearby Bradley International Airport. In short, the FAA completely lacked an explanation for the UFO that was witnessed and captured on film.

My next step was to send a copy of the photograph to the air force just to see what type of a response I would receive. Two weeks later, I received a call from a Lieutenant Colonel from the Air Defense Command, asking questions about the sighting. I was then politely instructed to turn over negatives and all prints to the air force for further analysis. When I declined, the officer became more aggressive and stated something about the National Security Act. I informed him that according to an official statement issued by the air force, UFOs presented no threat to national security and were therefore not included under that act. I informed him that the image was confirmed as a UFO by the FAA and since the air force had officially terminated their study on the subject, it had no jurisdiction regarding sightings or photographs. The officer told me they would send a special courier to pick up the negatives and prints. I replied, "Excuse me sir, but you just don't get it! I will not turn over anything that involves this particular case to the air force, or any other agency for that matter." Well, to make a very long story short, there were two more calls and four letters sent from different people in the air force and Naval Intelligence, but no one ever showed up at my door, and after three months, the calls and letters stopped entirely. Given the air force's numerous attempts to engage me, I decided that to release information on this case may not be such a good idea; I kept everything in my files for more than thirty years.

## The Emergence of the Black Triangles

Sightings of disc-like objects gave UFOs the name "flying saucers," and from 1947 to 1961, there were tens of thousands of reports from around the world. For the most part, sightings were uneventful; whatever was piloting these objects seemed benign and eager to keep its distance from humans, but that all changed when the black triangle-shaped UFOs began to appear. The late sixties to the present has seen a shift in the shape of UFOs from the disc or ellipse to a triangle. Today, triangle-shaped UFOs are being reported more frequently and, in my opinion, indicate an entirely different intelligence, evident in their increased aggression. Triangular UFOs are usually reported as black or "battleship gray" in color. When seen at night, they have multiple lights of different colors, at times so brilliant that witnesses describe the object as looking like a city or Christmas tree in the sky. I was the first one to document a major flap of these triangular UFOs in 1986 with the publication of my *Night Siege* book.[2] Since then, people from around the world have been sending me reports for my analysis because I am considered to be an "expert" of this type of UFO. To give my readers an idea of how aggressive these objects can be, I'll relate an encounter I investigated during the Hudson Valley flap when a triangular object hovered over the IPEC (Indian Point Energy Center) nuclear reactor in 1984. To my knowledge, this encounter is the only verified sighting of a UFO

2 A "flap" (sometimes a "UFO flap") is an outbreak of many UFO sightings over a relatively small geographical area.

over a nuclear complex where reactor operations were affected. The account below contains updated information that has never been released. I believe this account indicates beyond a shadow of a doubt that an alien intelligence was able to violate the security of one of the most heavily protected nuclear power plants in the United States.

### Aliens Buzz a Nuclear Reactor

The 1983 and 1984 sightings of UFOs in the Hudson River valley of New York were receiving a great deal of attention from local media. WNBC, a radio station in the greater New York area, asked me to come in to talk about the sightings. During the broadcast, I gave out my phone number and, shortly after the show ended, was barraged by calls.

After about two dozen calls, I received one I found very intriguing. The caller identified himself as a thirty-five-year-old New York State Power Authority police officer who worked as a security guard at the Indian Point nuclear reactor complex, located on the Hudson River in Buchanan, New York, just south of the town of Peekskill. The officer had been driving home from work when he caught the end of the talk show, and was anxious to talk with me. He told me that he was one of twelve officers who had seen the Hudson Valley UFO while on duty at the reactor complex. I had already received numerous sightings from people living near the plant who told me they had seen the UFO over the reactor, but I had very few details at the time. The person on the phone worked at the reactor complex; his responsibility was confirming these reports in addition to his other security-related duties. Although it's been twenty-five years, I still won't use his real name and reveal his identity. Nevertheless, the sighting at Indian Point remains the most incredible part of the Hudson Valley saga.

On the night of July 24, 1984, a giant triangular UFO hovered directly over one of the reactors at Indian Point for more than ten minutes. This was exciting because on July 24, a Brewster resident had videotaped the UFO from his back yard fifteen minutes before it appeared over the nuclear plant. I also had fourteen reports from various Peekskill residents who had seen the UFO hovering over the reactor area that night. This was excellent validation—a number of different sources could confirm the sighting over the reactor.

The security officer who called me was always referred to as "Carl" in my previous discussions concerning the Indian Point encounter. Carl informed me that he was going out on a limb and jeopardizing his career by coming forward with information about the sighting. He was convinced that what he and his fellow officers saw over the plant was something unconventional. They all felt fortunate, however, because they were able to get a real good look at the object as it hovered less than 300 feet above the exhaust tower at reactor number three. The event was so shocking, Carl said, that the shift commander was ready to give the order to shoot the UFO down.

When I asked Carl to meet me in person, he said he'd have to obtain clearance from his supervisor. The next day, he phoned and said his supervisor had cleared me to come to the reactor site on September 5 to speak with him and several other officers who had seen the object. He said no tape recorders or cameras would be allowed for security reasons, and I would have to submit to a routine check upon entering and leaving the security area. To make a very long story short, just before my appointment at Indian Point to interview the security people who had seen the UFO, I received a call from an individual from the New York Power Authority, stating that my request to visit the plant had been overturned and was now denied. The only reason this person gave me was that I might "compromise the security of a sensitive area." I contacted Carl at his home to let him know, and he didn't seem surprised. We arranged to meet at an out-of-the-way place outside the jurisdiction of Plant Operations and the NYPA. Carl told me that he would try to arrange for a number of other officers to join us, but couldn't promise anything.

### The Indian Point Report

The first interview took place at a place called the By-Pass Diner in Peekskill late on September 12, 1984, after the guards were off duty. Six of them showed up, and with assistance from investigators on my team, we were able to obtain detailed interviews from all of them. Carl talked to me for forty-five minutes that night, and would again on October 5, for a similar length of time. The first interview was taped, but not the second. Carl said there was certain information pertaining to plant security he did not want recorded.

Carl worked as a security officer for the Power Authority for three years and had been a New York state police officer before that. It turned out he'd had two sightings at the reactor complex: the first on June 14, and the other on July 24. His account in his own words is presented as follows:

"[On June 14,] I was on outside patrol at Indian Point Number Three. It was approximately quarter after ten at night, when I noticed out in the distance a series of lights low in the sky. We have a clear view for several miles in all directions, and I noticed these lights moving toward the direction of the facility; they were white with a yellow hue. I watched them for about ten minutes and estimated they were about a quarter of a mile from my position. They were approaching from the northeast, going southwest, coming directly toward the plant. At that point, I looked over at [the adjoining Consolidated-Edison nuclear power complex], and there were about ten of their security people looking at the same object. I got on the radio and called some of the other units to come out to my location to observe the object with me. I knew that it was something strange, and since it was getting so close, I wanted someone to come and assist me if I needed help. I didn't want to take any chances." Two other guards responded to his call.

"We all looked at this thing for approximately twenty minutes, and during that time, I would say it hovered in one area for about fifteen minutes without moving. The lights were incredibly bright and steady. It was hovering over the parking lot on the reactor grounds above some buildings that have lights on twenty-four hours a day. These are bright security lights, but the lights on this object were at least ten times as bright. The building it was over is quite large, about eighty feet high and this object dwarfed it. I estimated its size to be at least 300 feet from end to end, and it seemed to have a cone or triangle shape.

"As I watched, a plane passed over and when it passed above the object, the UFO blocked out the lights of the plane, and a few seconds later, the plane emerged from behind the other side of the object. So there was some type of huge, dark mass behind the lights. Then about fifteen minutes later, the object started to move, and when it did, it went very slow, no more than ten miles an hour. No small planes could stay in formation with the gusting wind that night.[3] The wind didn't faze these lights at all. When it hovered, it just stayed there, rock solid. I was in the service and flew helicopters, and know how hard it is to keep a formation with any type of aircraft in a high wind. No way was this a formation of planes. I saw no hint of any standard lights that a plane would have; also the lights were much too intense for a small aircraft. When the object turned, it rotated as if it was lying on a wheel. It made a very slow, sharp, ninety-degree turn. The object always moved in the direction of the apex, then after about ten minutes, it moved toward the Hudson and went north."

It seems the UFO didn't approach the high security area of the reactor that night, but that was to change when Carl told me about the incredible sighting that took place on the night of July 24, 1984, at 8:40 PM. His sighting account continues below.

---

3 A check with the National Weather Service indicated that the wind gusted to 25 knots that night, much too windy for planes to fly in formation.

"Another security guard called on his radio saying, 'Hey, here comes that UFO again!' With that being heard all over the air, everyone came running to see it. At that time, there were five of us, including two supervisors, who also came out to see it. It approached from basically the same direction as before, but this time, the lights were changing color. First, they would all be yellow, then white, and then they all turned blue. The lights were in a semicircle, and in the rear, pretty far back, was this red, blinking light.

"As the object approached the plant, it got as close as 500 feet from us. It looked like an ice cream cone. You could see it was a solid body about the size of three football fields. At this time, it was directly over our heads, and we were looking up at it. It was still moving, but very slowly. I could walk and keep up with it, so it must have been going slower than five to ten miles an hour. It took a long time to pass over, maybe five minutes. All this time, you could see the structure behind it. Only one of the three reactors was in operation—ours. This object picked the right one to fly over, and that's what got our supervisor worried. This thing got very close to the exhaust tower of reactor number three; no known aircraft can travel that slow, since the wind was also gusting that night.[4] We were all standing there with our mouths open and in complete awe of it! If the thing stayed over us, the order was already given to get ready to shoot it

---

4 A check with the National Weather Service indicated that the winds gusted to 30 miles per hour during the time of the sighting at Indian Point.

down. We had shotguns and were waiting for the final word to fire on it."

Another officer, who was on duty inside the security building, was watching the TV monitors at a console that allowed him to aim strategically placed cameras around and outside the buildings. During his interview he told me, "I received a call from two officers saying there was something in the sky, and I asked them what it was. They told me to swing my camera over in the direction where they were looking at this object. One of these cameras is at the top of a ninety-five-foot-tall pole. I turned this camera in that direction, and saw eight bright lights in a V shape, very wide, almost like a half circle. They were at least as bright as the landing lights on a large jet. My supervisor and I panned the camera up and down, and the object was very large, bigger than a football field. The object was so huge I had to pan the camera nearly 180 degrees to scan the entire object from front to back. It was one solid structure and was very large. We had it on camera for about fifteen minutes. I was trying to think of some logical explanation for what it was, but could not. Whatever it was, it was larger than a C-5A, the largest aircraft in the world, with a wingspan of 212 feet. This was much larger. It seemed very brazen. It acted like it didn't care who saw it."

Yet another officer, who was very reluctant to be taped for fear of jeopardizing his job, said, "There was this series of lights in the shape of a boomerang, and behind it was this dark structure, and there were these two things on the bottom that looked like hollow spheres of some sort. They looked like portals that could open up and rockets or something could fly out. The object was made up of some type of very dark material that only reflected a small part of the high-intensity security lights. It was very low and so close I actually got scared looking at it. I then pulled out my handgun, a 9mm pistol, and was getting ready to fire at it, but something popped into my head that this was a bad idea, so I put the gun back in my holster."

I would later meet one last time with Carl, whereupon I was informed that he could no longer discuss the sightings since his superiors knew about our meetings and was advised to stop. It seemed very strange to me that officials at the nuclear complex knew every detail about my secret meetings with Carl and his fellow officers. There is really no way they could have known, unless we were under some type of surveillance.

In December 1984, I tried to get the management of the reactor plant to discuss the UFO incidents, but they wouldn't cooperate. Gerry Culliton, then the news director for radio station WVIP in Mt. Kisco, New York, did get an acknowledgment from a Carl Patrick of the plant's information office that sightings did indeed take place. Culliton said, "Patrick told me there definitely were sightings, and the New York state police did an investigation and arrested four Cessna pilots. However, police records confirmed that no pilots were arrested on the nights in question or the days that followed." Culliton said he asked for a copy of the UFO incident report, but was told that "all security procedures and measures that are taken here are completely confidential to protect our own security." Culliton then asked Patrick, "Can you tell me if they fired on this thing?" Patrick replied, "I can neither confirm nor deny that the guards fired upon it, but they did what was necessary to protect the plant."

Shortly after the Culliton interview with Indian Point Spokesperson Carl Patrick, the *Journal News* (local Westchester paper) published a story called "Did Aliens Buzz Indian Point?" The story confirmed the information given to newsman Gerry Culliton; a spokesperson for Indian Point also confirmed the sighting.

I then filed five Freedom of Information Act requests with the New York Power Authority, the US Department of Energy, and the US Nuclear Regulatory Commission for any records relating to the UFO incidents; all replied that they had no documents.

My investigation of the Indian Point sightings took place before the publication of *Night Siege: The Hudson Valley UFO Sightings*, coauthored with Bob Pratt and the late Dr. J. Allen Hynek. However, information about the sightings at the plant continued to come my way years after the book's publishing, thanks to two contacts who held positions as secretaries inside the plant's security area.

One of these contacts told me that on numerous occasions, the night-shift workers saw short, gray-skinned alien-looking beings with large black eyes and tight-fitting black uniforms enter the reactor core area by walking through the walls. The aliens always appeared in pairs, at three in the morning. At least four sightings of these beings occurred over a six-month period. The beings seemed to have a shimmer around them as if encased by a force field, and one of them always carried an instrument it moved over the casing of the reactor core.

Soon after the UFO sightings, engineers at the plant discovered a crack in the reactor casing and an unexplainable power drain. Somehow, this story leaked out to the press and was the subject of a number of local newspaper and television stories. The power drain was of major concern, because Indian Point #3 supplies electricity to the NYC subway system and a number of "secret" NASA listening posts in the area. According to both of my contacts, a man dressed in civilian clothes identifying himself as "Colonel Roberts" came to the plant one afternoon and had a lengthy discussion with the plant administrator. Although my contact could not hear the conversation from her boss's office (whose door was left partially open), she was shocked when "Colonel Roberts" seemed to lose his temper, yelling, "I DON'T CARE IF THEY'RE FROM OUTER SPACE! SHOOT THE BASTARDS!"

Fallout

In 1985, I received a call from the New York state attorney general's office informing me that charges were being filed against me for violating the National Security Act. The attorney who called me stated they had proof I was given information from the officers at the Indian Point nuclear plant that were vital to the protection of that facility. The attorney was aware I was getting ready to publish a book on the UFO sightings, and warned me that any reference to Indian Point would be considered a violation of security. Several days later, I received an official letter from the Nuclear Regulatory Commission stating that I would be required to come to a hearing; they felt that the safety of that reactor had been compromised. And if *that* wasn't enough, one week later, I received a letter from the National Security Agency, who tried to pressure me to not release any information about the sightings at the reactor in the not-yet-published nor -written book everyone seemed to know about. There were even calls made from the governor's office and the state police to the principal of the school where I was teaching science, informing them of "possible criminal charges" for my involvement in obtaining classified information without proper authority or clearance. Needless to say, this was a very rough time in my life—at least once a week, I received some type of threatening phone call or letter.

The Indian Point incident was covered up successfully, but I still had the videotape of the UFO taken by a Brewster resident less than twenty minutes before the security people at the nuclear facility saw it. I also had recorded statements from the security officers stating that the sighting was something that couldn't be conventionally explained. The official explanation of the sighting is that it was nothing more than a group of prankster pilots flying small aircraft in a very tight formation. The July 24 Brewster video was sent to the Jet Propulsion Laboratory in Pasadena, California. JPL does the imaging for the space program and has in its ranks the top imaging scientists in the country, if not the world. JPL is also one of the most anti-UFO organizations in the world. I wanted to know if the lights in the video represented one solid object or a number of smaller objects (planes) close together. A letter from the Director of JPL at that time, Dr. Lew Allen, stated: "The lights in the video represent one ridged object." This would rule out the planes-in-formation theory, which by the way has never been seriously considered by anyone who saw this UFO.

In 1992, the television show *Unsolved Mysteries* presented the Hudson Valley UFO sightings on prime time television, but didn't include the Indian Point sightings. In 1993, I was contacted by one of the show's directors, who told me they were planning on doing a special show about the reactor complex encounter. The director even came out to survey the area; they planned to film a re-enactment at an abandoned reactor in Pennsylvania. Two weeks before the scheduled shooting, the producers got a call from some powerful government agency, and the filming was cancelled. Neither the director nor I was ever given a reason why the episode's filming was cancelled or who made the call. Whoever the agency was, they had enough power to shut down a very well-known Hollywood production company. It's hard for me to believe that there are all these so-called UFO investigators out there who claim to have been able to get classified information regarding UFOs without having ever suffered any consequences. I had just touched on an area of national security involving a UFO sighting over a nuclear reactor and got my ears pinned back almost instantly!

## A Change in Behavior

While most would assume every UFO behaves similarly, if not identically, there is a wealth of evidence pointing to the contrary. I could go on at length about the difference in behavior between the discs and the triangles. When approached, the intelligence behind the "flying saucers" seems to keep its distance, wanting to avoid confrontation. In contrast, the triangles go out of their way to violate high security areas and airspace. The intelligence that operates this type of craft seems to have a much more advanced technology than the disc pilots, and their interactions with the human race—especially during a contact experience—are not always benign. For years, people have reported various levels of contact with beings described as short, having large heads, eyes, and grayish or clay-like skin. Since the first appearance of the triangles, many of these reports of contact encounters have changed. A new type of being has appeared on the scene: more insectoid or reptilian in appearance and definitely more terrifying than its gray counterparts. Do they represent two different species? Are they both extraterrestrial? Is one of them not from our reality, but from another dimension or universe? One thing is certain: behavior of the two is very different. The Grays seem to have concern for the humans they abduct but the insectoids and reptilians treat us like laboratory specimens. In the coming chapters, I will explore the contact phenomenon in greater detail and hope to shed more light on these questions.

# TWO

# THE HIDDEN EPIDEMIC

With the appearance of the black triangles, the UFO abduction stories not only changed, but signaled the emergence of creatures referred to as the "Reptilians." In the fifties, movies about trips to Venus and Mars featuring beautiful, benevolent space aliens were wildly popular; most Americans laughed at these stories because they provided a more lighthearted look at the UFO situation. However, as we approached the sixties, these stories turned from trips to outer space with the "space brothers" (and sisters) to tales of being kidnapped by aliens who were not little *green* men, but *gray*. It seemed the purpose of the abduction was to perform scientific experiments on human beings. Despite the fact that humans were abducted against their will, the contact seemed benevolent for the most part, since abductees were never harmed and usually brought home safely. With the appearance of the black triangles, the scenario changed considerably: the abducting aliens looked more like monsters and seemed to have no regard for the well-being of their captured humans. Are all the people abducted by these "aliens" brought back home? No one knows for sure. According to the FBI, thousands of people disappear every year without a trace. If we take into consideration that 90 percent are murdered or runaways, there are still a considerable number of people who seemingly vanish from the face of the Earth for no reason at all. Where have they gone? Is it possible that this newer alien intelligence is taking them and not bringing them back? If these aliens are here already, what do the governments of the world have to say about it? The United States government, for one, denies the existence of UFOs, aliens, and anything else that may not be Earth- or manmade. The United States Air Force officially stopped investigating UFO reports in 1969, yet documents obtained from the Freedom of Information Act revealed that all branches of the military and intelligence agencies have continued to collect encounters with UFOs long after their release and official declaration that they were no longer collecting reports.

In the past twenty years, I have been personally contacted by the following agencies in the government regarding my UFO research: the United States Air Force, the National Security Agency, the Federal Bureau of Investigation, and the Central Intelligence Agency. During the Hudson Valley UFO sightings, all the agencies mentioned above wanted to know *exactly* what I discovered about the sightings and what documented proof was in my possession. This is quite a contradiction to the government's official policy regarding the UFO phenomenon . . . if UFOs don't exist (as they claim), why are they still interested in sightings?

## Triangles in the Sky: Sightings from 1986 to 2008

Sightings of the black triangles are not limited to North America—they've been seen on a worldwide scale. The most celebrated cases are the Hudson Valley sightings, the Belgium flap, and the Phoenix lights. These UFO flaps are considered classic because they involved hundreds of witnesses. I suggest my readers peruse the case material; the documentation represents three of the most well-documented UFO sightings in history. The Hudson Valley sightings were the first modern-day sightings of the dark triangle involving hundreds of witnesses. Because I was one of the original investigators of this case, I became some kind of unofficial "expert" on UFOs of this type. As a result, I received hundreds of reports describing encounters with triangular UFOs. Following are some of the more interesting reports I have received over the years.

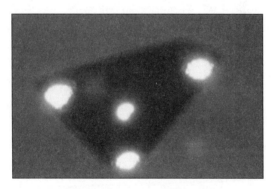

*A dark triangle UFO over Belgium, 1998*
*(Photo Credit: Société Belge d'Etude des*
*Phénomènes Spatiaux [SOBEPS])*

*1986*

Wilmington and Hampstead, NC: On April 5, a 53-year-old woman and her husband were returning home to Hampstead after dining in Wilmington, when they saw lights about 400 feet above US-17. It was a boomerang- or triangle-shaped object as big as two football fields. "It just came over really slow[ly]. We estimated its speed at about 15 to 20 miles per hour," said the woman. The object then projected down a blinding beam of white light from its underside. As the light went out, the man got out of the car and looked up at it. His wife said, "I believe it was the most terrifying feeling I've ever had in my life. I caught myself trying to hide from the lights behind my husband. I begged him to get back in the car, but it was like he was mesmerized. It scared me so badly, I cried. It left me with a very uneasy feeling, a very humble feeling. I didn't want to see anything like that again."

Afterwards, the man began having dreams of aliens with scaly skin and reptile-like eyes. While relaxing in the evening, he would often doodle symbols in some unknown language and images of places that didn't seem to be part of our world. His wife said that while sleeping, her husband would often speak words she thought sounded like Latin. After waking him up, he would have no recollection of what he said.

Kremmling, Dillon, and Silverthorne, CO: Sometime during the night of April 20 in these mountainous regions of Colorado, local officials in two counties received calls about stationary lights in the sky. One Kremmling police officer saw the lights and then was informed of sightings over the Green

Mountain Reservoir near the Grand-Summit county line. He hurried there and found a large group of officers from both counties watching the lights. Through a high-powered telescope, the object appeared to be triangular, with lights along the outer edges. There was also some unidentifiable black mass connecting the lights, blocking out the stars. The object, estimated to be the size of two football fields, hovered motionless for a while and then took off to the southwest. The most starling aspect of the occurrence was the evasive maneuver taken by a jet plane also in the area, which all those who were present saw veer around the object. The Kremmling police officer said the group watched the lights for about two hours.

Waukesha, WI: On November 24, at 11 PM, a twenty-nine-year-old-man saw flashing red lights in the sky to the southeast while driving home. He thought at first that they were lights on a radio station tower but as he got closer, he could see the lights were spinning around, like police car lights. "But it was up in the sky, no more than 200 feet high, hovering in the air and rotating," he said. He stopped in a parking lot about 150 yards away from the object, exited his vehicle, and watched in utter amazement.

The object was shaped like a flattened triangle and was perhaps seventy-five feet wide. At each corner were pairs of flashing red lights. On the sides were pairs of white and red lights that did not flash. The craft seemed to be dark brown or black in color. As it hovered, it rotated slowly and noiselessly. After two or three minutes, the man decided to get a closer look, but as he drove closer, the lights stopped rotating and the object began moving away at a very low altitude, staying in front of him. The object then headed over a grove of trees, and the man lost sight of it.

### *1987*

Devil's Lake, ND: On March 9, 1987, sometime between 8:30 and 11 PM, a number of residents, including two off-duty police officers, saw a diamond-shaped, multicolored object that hovered and moved quickly over the area. The two officers watched the object for fifteen to twenty minutes. It had red, yellow, and green lights that appeared to blink or possibly rotate. The object hovered at an altitude of about 500 feet, but left in a "quick manner that was considerably faster than any plane."

Hutchinson, KS: In the same year, on April 17, at 10:20 PM, a couple sitting on their porch saw a triangular object "gliding by," going east. It had no lights and made no noise. "We couldn't see it until the street lights reflected on it," said the wife. "It was like a boomerang with the apex pointed forward. It was hard to tell how big it was." The color was "gunmetal blue," according to the husband, who was certain it wasn't a plane. As the object approached their home, it seemed to slow down, at which point both people thought they heard a voice inside their head saying, "We have come a long way and, not having found what we are looking for, shall leave." The object then disappeared in a puff of white smoke. The smoke turned into a thick cloud and drifted away.

Worthing, West Sussex, England: On October 21, at 9 PM, two men reported seeing a glowing object in the sky. One, a car salesman, said it was "hovering, looking at first like a shaft of light, right in the middle of the sky. It seemed to change shape from a rugby ball, to a hemisphere, triangle, then a square. Then, it gradually shrank into a red dot and disappeared. It was about the size of a low full moon." The other man said: "It was amorphous and kept changing shape, I have never experienced anything like it before and we saw it clearly for twenty to twenty-five minutes." Two days later, an eighteen-year-old insurance clerk spotted a strange yellow light over the same area. "It sort of stretched as if it was trying to break apart—it was as though some invisible hand was playing with soft, hot plastic." In this case as with many others, we see the triangular craft's ability to traverse dimensions.

### 1988

Porterville, CA: During the night of October 26, 1988, hundreds of people in the area reported seeing strange objects in the sky. Among the witnesses was a couple and their son, sitting in the back of their pickup truck at a drive-in movie. "We could see individual lights," the wife said. "There were five separate objects, each was V-shaped with one a little ahead of the other. Red and white lights were along the Vs, with a large red light at the back of each object." Another witness said: "There were a series of red lights behind the main object. I would say three lights. When it flew in front of the moon, there weren't any wings and it glided very silently." Other witnesses speculated the craft could be a stealth bomber, but officials at nearby Northrop Corporation denied any of their craft were flying that night. The only other airstrip in the area is Castle Air Force Base; only the considerably noisy B-52s fly out of there.

Lajas and Cabo Rojo, Puerto Rico: On December 28, 1988, hundreds of people reported that they had seen jet fighters chase a small UFO over the Sierra Bermeja, a small mountain ridge near these towns, earlier that day. At 7:45 that evening, they saw a large triangular UFO that seemed to have some kind of extended appendage on its front section with many brilliant colored lights blinking continuously. The object was slightly curved at its rear end and was composed of a gray metallic substance, with a large central yellow light emitting from a bulging, luminous, concave appendage. At the triangle's right "wing tip" were brilliant yellow lights and on the left, red ones. As the people watched, two jet fighters tried to intercept it. They passed in front of it, whereupon the UFO veered to the left and made a turn back, reducing its speed. The jets tried to intercept it three times, when suddenly the UFO decreased its speed again, almost stopping in midair as if to confront them. One jet stationed itself at the right side of the UFO and the other at its rear. Suddenly, the jet in back just disappeared on top or inside the UFO (the witness was watching with binoculars and never saw the jet emerge from beyond the UFO). The second jet remained very close to the right side of the object, looking very small in comparison. As the UFO flew a little to the west, the second jet also disappeared. The witnesses were sure it was taken inside the giant triangular craft. When this happened, all witnesses reported being unable to hear any noise from the jet engines. After trapping the jets, the object lowered its position and came very close to the ground over a small body of water known as Saman Lake. It hovered there for a moment, straightened its corners, and emitted a flash of yellow light from its central ball of light. The object then divided itself into two different distinct triangular sections. The triangle on the right was illuminated in yellow, and the left, red. Both shot off at great speed: one to the southeast, the other to the northwest. Red sparks could be seen falling when the object divided itself. A retired army veteran living in the area said that at 8:20 PM, a group of black helicopters arrived and flew over the Sierra Bermeja and the Laguna Cartagena area without lights until midnight, appearing to be searching for something. I later checked with all Puerto Rican and US government agencies that might have knowledge of the incident, but all denied knowing anything about the sighting and the jets' encounter with the UFO. A Mr. Jorge Martín of Rio Piedras said that a week later, a naval officer whom he could not identify confirmed the encounter and said that the jets and their pilots were taken by the UFO. He said that radar tapes had been sent to Washington, DC, and that a lid of secrecy had been placed on the whole affair. Shortly after the incident, the local government "leased" the area of the Sierra Bermeja and Laguna Cartagena to the federal government, reportedly because the government was building a Voice of America radio station there. The Voice of America is an international short-wave radio broadcasting system that is operated secretly by the CIA and used to promote pro-America sentiments. However, no station was ever built, and what they were really doing in that area remains a mystery to this day.

## 1989

Long Island, NY: January 30, 1989. In the predawn hours at Montauk Harbor on January 30, a thirty-foot fishing boat had an encounter with a UFO near the surface of the water just after rounding Shagwong Point en route to cod-fishing waters. For about ten minutes, the captain watched a strange light on the water just north of the Montauk lighthouse. The light seemed to come from an unknown object in the sky. The captain changed course slightly and began to head toward the light. At first, he thought it was a helicopter, but when he neared the light, he was surprised to hear no sound. He also noticed that in addition to his on-board radar system, a number of electronic devices had stopped working. Apprehensive, the captain killed the boat's running lights and engine. To him and his two crewmen, the light appeared to be square-shaped and was less than a mile away. Suddenly, the light began moving toward the boat, bobbing around and moving from side to side as it came closer. "I really thought it was going to stop right over us," the captain said. As it neared, he noticed the object was triangular or diamond-shaped and about 150 feet in length. The only noise emanating from it was a slight humming sound. "It turned belly-up and cruised west and then south, climbing higher and higher until it disappeared," the captain said. As soon as the UFO vanished, the radar and electronics were once again functional.

Easton and Trumbull, CT: On May 4, from 9:30 to 10 PM, a resident reported seeing an object shaped like a flying wing with red, yellow, and blue lights in the rear and a blinking red light on the right side. It flew over the tree line behind his house. A woman in Trumbull reported seeing a low-flying V-shaped object as big as a football field accompanied by a faint hum. The object had many colored lights and looked like a Christmas tree in the sky. At about 10 PM, an engineer driving to his home in Trumbull saw a cluster of three concentrated, bright red and white lights. He decided it was a helicopter, but thought it was peculiar. It was traveling slowly toward Bridgeport, just to the south. The engineer stopped and the red and white lights disappeared, the object now looking like a blue boomerang with soft blue lights. Intrigued, he went home and phoned his father, who had worked for the Sikorsky helicopter company for fifteen years, and lived up the street. The UFO was still in the sky and the man's father, who could identify any helicopter by sound, told his son that "this was no helicopter." The two followed the object to a closed golf course where it disappeared in the sky. The father was unable to identify the craft. "I can't find a feasible answer," the engineer said. "It would have taken a tremendous amount of money and energy to do this. I did some triangulation, and was able to figure out that the object was between eight hundred and thirteen hundred feet above my head. The lights changed color and a blue 'V' formed out of nowhere. I don't know how someone could pull this off, or why they would want to."

Police in both Easton and Trumbull received several phone calls reporting UFO sightings that night. One report came from a woman in Easton who said the object passed over her front yard, and when it did, a bright blue light projected to the ground. As she watched, she saw figures that looked like large people glide down the light then back up into the ship.

She watched this for about two minutes before the blue light went out and the object moved away noiselessly. Easton is close to the Hudson Valley, where similar sightings describing a projected blue light from a UFO had also occurred between 1983 and 1987.

Winnipeg, Manitoba, Canada: From 11:15 PM to 2:15 AM on October 9, an amateur astronomer waiting for an anticipated meteor shower reported to the Manitoba Planetarium that he had sighted nine unidentified objects as follows: 11:20 to 11:30 PM, a large boomerang-shaped object flew north to south over the city; 11:35 PM, three ball-shaped objects flew along the same path, followed by another boomerang-shaped object going east to west; 12:07 AM, three more ball-shaped objects flew over the city in a straight line, with a fourth trailing off slightly to the west; 1:08 AM, another boomerang flew north to south, but lower in the sky. The witness said he was sure these weren't planes or satellites. "I used to help build planes and I've seen lots of satellites," he said. "These things had no lights. They were strictly self-illuminated objects. They were very clear and very sharp." Ed Barker, the planetarium producer and director of the Manitoba Centre for UFO Studies, said the planetarium had received a number of calls at the end of the summer regarding boomerang-shaped objects in the sky.

## 1990

Newburgh, NY: Located about sixty miles from New York City, Newburgh marks the center of the Hudson River Valley. From June to December, a dark triangle-shaped UFO was

seen moving silently over the back country and heavily populated city area. The number of people who saw this object
was in the hundreds—perhaps the thousands. This number
is based on reports made to police, newspapers, radio stations, and UFO researchers, including myself. As in other
encounters/sightings, the object had bright multi-colored
lights around its edges and three to six lights underneath.
It was reported to have been at least two hundred feet from
end to end and appeared very thin. At times, the light would
hover above a house or car and project down a brilliant beam
of white light. Some witnesses felt a type of "psychic communication" with the object. Later, many of these people
would report having contact or abduction experiences with
alien intelligence.

## 1991

North Central Connecticut: On May 23, area residents observed a large, dark triangle in the sky. The object was seen
over I-91 near Hartford and caused a traffic jam, as motorists
slowed down to get a better look at it. The *Hartford Courant*
reported the object was responsible for at least three fender
benders as startled drivers slammed on their brakes while
the UFO passed over their car at an altitude of no more than
five hundred feet. The object was also seen at Bradley International Airport by air traffic controllers who reported
plain, naked-eye sightings of the object, but no matching radar activity. The next day, Connecticut state police said the
sighting was caused by a number of prankster stunt pilots
who had tried to fake a UFO in New York eight years earlier.

However, people who saw the UFO said it was unlike any known aircraft they had ever seen before; the object looked like it was from another world. After this sighting, I spoke with nine people who witnessed the object while on I-91; all were normal, professional people who described the encounter as frightening and amazing.

### 1992

Palm Springs, CA; Phoenix, AZ; Fort Worth, TX: While driving on eastbound I-10 (about halfway to Phoenix) on October 5, at approximately 10:30 PM, two witnesses observed a large triangular "vessel" passing over their vehicle. "It was *huge*, bigger than a stealth bomber and it moved *so* slow . . . much slower than any airplane, with no sound at all. It was about three hundred feet above us. It wasn't smooth on the bottom, and because there was a dim blue glow, you could see different areas of its underbelly. There were other cars behind us, and I'm sure they saw what we saw. The UFO then turned and shot away. We both turned to each other and said, 'No one will believe us!'"

The following report below took place on the same date and time, but in Texas. The report was emailed to me after the witness read one of my books.

"My husband and I were outside walking, talking, and looking at the stars. We were in a residential neighborhood, the houses being on at least one-acre lots, all of which have trees on them. We are twenty-five miles west of downtown Fort Worth, and there were no street lights, so you could see the stars very well. From where we were standing, in the street, you couldn't really see the horizon, just the houses and trees around us. Suddenly, from what appeared to be only a few feet above the trees (moving north to south), a large, black (or dark gray) aircraft came into view. I can't remember what the 'front' of it looked like, just that there was something very large approaching us. It was totally silent. No vibration, no air movement, no smell, no visible moving parts, no smoke, nothing! I got the impression that it was either rectangular, or maybe triangular, and for some reason I was thinking that it had to be pretty flat. It hovered directly over us and when we looked up, the aircraft filled our field of vision completely. You couldn't see the stars or sky behind it. It seems there were some faint white lights on the edges of it, but we never did agree on what the lights looked like, or if there were even lights at all. The whole encounter lasted under a minute. I don't remember how it left our field of vision, and neither can my husband. Nothing can fly that low, slow and quiet, without crashing to the ground, not to mention the immense size of it. What is almost as weird as the sighting itself, is that my husband and I never could be more specific about what we saw, it was as if it all went blank in our mind."

### 1993

Location Unknown: The following report was sent to me in 1994 and although the witness didn't give his name or the sighting's location, I still believe it should be included here.

"It was a dark windy November night years ago, but the vision still haunts me. I was sixteen back then, and was in the forest with a friend, having some fun. At our usual fire spot, we saw a couple of lights through the trees—I thought they were from a road nearby, but I wasn't sure. My friend fired six starter gun blanks in the air and suddenly, the lights started to ascend over the trees! Now panicking, we saw that the lights were from a big, black, triangular object. It hovered just over trees and flew over us very slowly and very silently. The wind stopped, making it seem like this thing 'created' silence. We panicked and started to run like crazy. When we finally found a clear spot, we were spotted by a kind of searchlight . . . it was the object! We had just run a forty-five-minute walk in less than ten minutes. We were convinced the aliens were going to abduct us. Then, everything went black, and we were back at the camp. The fire was out and three hours of time had passed. The next day, a couple of army helicopters flew very low over the area where me and my friend's encounter happened. Writing [to the author] is the first time I've filed a report on the encounter—no one believed us at the time, and we were afraid to go to the government with our story."

## 1994

Benton County, MO: On October 1 at around 9 PM, four people were traveling together on state highway T in a southerly direction. As they topped a hill, heading towards the Tebo Bridge, everyone witnessed a light hovering above the water on the bridge's east side. One of the people in the vehicle made a comment about what it might be. They continued in a southerly direction and came upon the bridge and stopped their vehicle. All four people exited the vehicle and stood there watching the light hovering approximately fifty feet above the bridge and approximately one-eighth mile east of the bridge. The main witness told me, "The best way to describe this light would be that it was similar to lights you'd see on an airplane, but this was a constant light, not flashing or anything of the sort. This object was below the ridge line that ran in an east-northeastern direction with the water, so I'm confident in my distance estimation between us and the object. It was very dark, and it was difficult to see the craft's outline."

The weather was calm and they noticed a complete silence—this craft made no noise. After the object hovered above the water for approximately ten minutes, it turned and pointed in a northerly direction. As it turned to the north, the group saw another light on the craft's rear. However, since it was so dark outside, they had a difficult time making out the object's profile, but all three witnesses said it appeared to be triangle-shaped. After the craft turned, it slowly and silently moved to the north, and was soon lost from sight.

## 1995

Sinfin Moor, Spondon, and Barrow-upon-Trent, Derby; King's Newton, Hampshire, England: For the past fifteen years, residents of Derby, England, have been plagued with a series of sightings they have nicknamed the "Flying Triangles." In the early morning hours of March 16, two brothers were driving along Route A52 near Willington, South Derbyshire. They were on their way to Swarkestone and had just gone around a tight bend in the road when they saw a very large triangular object coming directly towards them. It had approximately nine large three-dimensional light panels that looked like blocks of white light underneath the aircraft. Because of the intensity, it was very difficult to make out any outlines while it was overhead, but it appeared to be a type of delta wing. The brothers stopped the car and got out to watch for several minutes, but the cold weather prevented them from staying out for an extended period of time. While watching the craft travel very slowly, both men wondered why it didn't stall and lose altitude. They were able to hear a sound like a jet engine and figured it was some kind of night surveillance craft.

The very next night, the same object was seen by a couple in the Sinfin Moor, Derby area—their first encounter with the "Flying Triangle." The wife said one could "see it very clearly; it was very low and slowly moving right over the rooftops. I couldn't believe it—I was flabbergasted. It was massive, bigger than a plane. [My husband and I] weren't frightened, just fascinated." The husband was to see it again on April 4 at about one o'clock in the morning. This time, the object was stationary for a long period of time, and moved even slower than before. It was again noiselessly gliding along, and featured red and white lights.

On Wednesday, April 26, at 11:45 PM, a language teacher was getting ready to go to bed when she noticed an illuminated aircraft approaching her home. She lives on Stenson Road, Derby, near the East Midlands Airport, so she was accustomed to seeing low-flying aircraft over her house. However, this one was different—it was heading in from the wrong direction, and seemed black and huge. As it got closer, the woman was able to make out the shape of a large, black, triangular craft. It had a white light in each corner and a red flashing light almost in the center. The woman was able to hear a faint engine noise, but it didn't sound anything like a typical jet aircraft. She got a clear view of the underside and noticed it was definitely triangular, quite sharply defined, lacking wings and a tail.

The UFO would make another appearance on April 28 in the Spondon, Derby section. An area resident was driving along Route A52 in the direction of Nottingham, about four miles outside of Derby. It was eight o'clock when he noticed a low moving light in the sky. Because of the turns in the road, the witness was unable to give the strange craft any real attention, but when he pulled off the road at a junction and looked for the lights again, he saw them. The lights appeared as an equilateral triangle, not very brilliant, but all had the same brightness. The "flying triangle" was traveling point-first with a pulsating red light visible off-center underneath it. The man was also able to make out a dim green light in the back, but it could only be seen at a distance. He watched the object for about thirty seconds as it slowly passed on his driver's side, and then, tried to roll down the window to get a better view. He thought he was able to make out a triangular silhouette against the sky, but he was unable to hear any sound.

The man used to live near the East Midlands Airport and was familiar with low-flying aircraft. The object's lights were much too dim to be landing lights and were not on the craft's wing tips, like on a plane. He thought it might be a helicopter, but the two rear lights were too far apart, and helicopters make a great deal of noise.

On May 1, a member of the Southern Paranormal Investigations Group based in Hampshire had a surprise sighting. Darren Collins was visiting friends on vacation in a place called Kings Newton. As he prepared to leave for home, his friends told him that if he cut through a little lane up ahead, he would come out on Route 514, the way he needed to go. As he approached the junction of 514, a number of lights in a field caught his attention. He immediately thought, "I am *not* going to miss this!" He pulled over and got out of the car, left it running, and quickly walked about a hundred yards up the road. The object was floating in the air, absolutely still, and seemed to be triangular in shape. There were lights in each corner, and a flashing, red off-center light. Darren couldn't believe what he was seeing. There was no way this thing was a plane, because prior to this sighting he had just seen one, and this object was only about six hundred yards away and a hundred and fifty feet in the air. Darren stood for about two minutes, caught up in the wonder of the experience, when, for whatever reason, he decided to shout at it to "come here! Come over here!" He doesn't know if it was coincidence or not, but the object moved slightly to the right and then "took off with great acceleration," disappearing from his view in three seconds. The object had flown off in the direction of Barrow-upon-Trent, a smaller Derby city, going northeast.

*1996*

Wethersfield, CT: Although this central Connecticut town is close to the stomping ground of the giant triangle UFO seen over the northeast United States from 1982 to 1995, only one incident was reported from this location, just south of Hartford. On July 24, at about 8:30 PM, residents called police to report a large object with bright lights slowly passing over the town—it didn't make a sound and was apparently losing altitude. The local authorities first sent out a number of patrol cars, fearing it was a large commercial aircraft in trouble, headed for an emergency landing at Bradley Airport. When police caught sight of the object, they realized it was completely unlike any aircraft they had seen before. Reports from that night indicate that the UFO was at least two hundred feet from end to end, and was shaped like a dark triangle with three lights on the bottom that were red, green, and blue. The red light was on the end of the object and blinked repeatedly. The dark triangle continued its flight over the town and occasionally stopped in midair to project a faint blue beam of light to the ground, engulfing a house or car parked on the road. Of the dozen or so witnesses I interviewed, all indicated the unknown aircraft flew very low and was quite large. Hartford police were convinced it was some type of experimental military aircraft, but despite calls made to the FAA and the local Air National Guard, they were unable to receive any definite answers about the object's origin. As a dozen or so witnesses watched, the object gained another thousand feet or so of altitude.

Startled residents continued to watch as two military jet aircraft entered the vicinity and circled the object, passing close by on the left and right. People came out of their homes, got out of cars, and lined up on the streets to watch the strange dance between the UFO and the two military jets. Then the object froze in midair and all the lights went out. When this happened, witnesses observing the UFO from the ground said the object looked like a dark mass and blocked out the area's usual light pollution. As they watched the UFO, the sound of helicopters could be heard in the distance. No more than two minutes had passed when the choppers approached the object from the west. One of them flew directly above the UFO, hovered there, and dropped a magnesium flare, briefly lighting up the sky and ground. One witness told me, "The amazing thing was, despite the flare being so bright, all it did was make the outline of the UFO more pronounced against the sky. The flare didn't illuminate any structure on the object—it was still jet black." This an interesting comment because in many cases involving this type of UFO, the triangle's building material acts almost like a black body, absorbing the light that hits it, reflecting very little in the visible spectrum. The helicopters and jets retreated, and soon after, the UFO seemed to fold down on itself and vanish.

This report was similar to one that had taken place in 1984 in Danbury, Connecticut. A dark triangle was reported hovering over the Danbury Fair Mall and was witnessed by hundreds of shoppers and eight Danbury police officers. During the sighting, a helicopter came into the area and hovered above the object, whereupon it dropped a bright flare that illuminated the ground below, but not the object. As the flare died out, at least nine more helicopters arrived and approached the UFO. As if in response to the helicopters' arrival, the object gained altitude and vanished above the cloud cover, which was four thousand feet at the time. Witnesses, including the police officers, said that the helicopters did not pursue the UFO. A check with the Air National Guard revealed that the helicopters came from the Danbury Airport, and were responding to a report of a low-altitude aircraft. The above was the only information the officer at flight operations had (or was willing to give me).

## 1997

Thomaston, CT: On March 26 just before 8:30 PM, police in Thomaston and surrounding towns received calls about an aircraft at low altitude, possibly in trouble. As the lights approached, residents realized what was approaching was no ordinary type of aircraft they had ever seen. Witnesses that contacted me directly or made calls to the local police described the object as a dark triangle, perhaps two hundred feet in length, from the apex to the rear. The triangular craft had six lights on the bottom: one in the front, amber in color; three across the middle which were blue, yellow, and green; and two at each point in the rear, both red. The object moved silently over the streets and homes at less than eight hundred feet in altitude and, according to newspaper accounts published the next day, created a near panic. Witnesses who stood directly under the UFO said it was so huge and low that it took a long time to pass over. Looking up, they noticed the dark mass black out the clear night sky. The object occasionally projected down a brilliant beam of white light that engulfed entire houses and cars. One witness told me that when the light covered his car, he had to pull over because it caused a complete white-out. This witness, in addition to others who were bathed in the light, claimed they felt some type of contact with the object; some had images appear in their minds of alien-like creatures, while others claimed to have heard a voice speak in an unknown language. The UFO silently floated away but was not reported north of Hartford. Where did it go? It seemed to have disappeared without a trace, yet there are no witnesses who saw it vanish in the sky.

### The Triangles and Their Fascination with Bodies of Fresh Water

I consider myself pretty fortunate to live close to many of these triangular UFO sightings; I've been able to collect accurate reports on other data shortly after events have taken place.

When the UFOs appeared in the Hudson River Valley, they took a definite path: they would proceed north, loop around to the east (toward Connecticut), and always head west to vanish in the Kent Cliffs area of Putnam County. When the triangles were seen in this county, they were often reported hovering around or above the numerous bodies of water in that area. These bodies of water are mostly reservoirs for New York City, but some of them are natural lakes produced in the last ice age, eighteen thousand years ago. I was very interested in these lake sightings because my past research had shown that some of them are the location of strong magnetic anomalies. I had hundreds of UFO reports, so it was easy to select those cases which took place near or above a body of water. I selected 512 cases; they were then broken down into various categories, listed below.

Sightings above the water (1,000 feet or more): 292 cases

Sightings at low altitude near the water (between 100 and 200 feet): 96 cases

Sightings at very low altitude (at water level, and less than 50 feet): 124 cases

I decided to focus on reports that indicated the UFO was fifty feet or less above water level. In many of the 124 cases selected, there seemed to be some type of interaction between the UFO and the water. Also, in all 512 cases, the UFO was reported to be triangular in shape and two hundred feet or less in size. To give you an idea of some of the encounters, I will present three cases below.

### A Reservoir Encounter

The witness, John Falk, has a background in engineering and had never before witnessed a UFO or experienced any type of paranormal phenomenon. On March 19, 1983, he was driving home from work on Route 100, passing by the New Croton Falls Reservoir, located near Yorktown in Westchester County. It was two in the morning and the road was quite deserted. Suddenly, John noticed a dark mass hovering above the water, completely still. At first, John didn't think too much of it because he was on his way home from work and was very tired, but something told him this object's behavior was quite unusual. John pulled his car over to the side of the road and turned his lights off. He sat in his car for several minutes and watched the object as it hovered no more than fifteen feet above the water, in total silence. The object was much darker than the light-polluted sky, so he was able to see that it was triangular in shape and very large. He was about five to seven hundred feet from the UFO and was parked near Muscoot Farm Park, which at the time was a very dark section of road.

After several minutes, John noticed the object starting to move. When it did, a row of red lights appeared up and down the chevron of the triangle. John told me the color of the lights was very similar to that of a helium-neon laser (a very bright red) and he was amazed at how pure the red came through. The object then began moving very slowly around the water, and as John rolled down his window, he was amazed that any aircraft of that size could move so slowly without making a sound. John wondered if this strange craft might be some type of experimental government doing research in the area, but decided this thing was not of this Earth. How he knew this, he doesn't know. He told me, "It was just a feeling that came over me while I watched it move and saw those lights; I knew it was not of human design." He got out of his car, walked through a wooded area, stood at the reservoir's edge, and watched as the object slowly drifted towards him. The UFO was now no more than two hundred feet from him and he was able to see it was made up of some type of very dark gray material. The object seemed very smooth and he could not see any joints or sections. Except for the red lights, most of the object was dark, but John could also see a faint red glow that seemed to come from the underside of the UFO, reflecting off the water.

As he continued to watch the UFO, a car approached the reservoir area. As the car's headlights came closer, the lights on the UFO went out; all that was visible was a dark mass which would have been barely noticeable from the road. As the car passed, the lights on the object lit up again and the UFO resumed its sweeping behavior over the water, which it repeated three more times during the twenty-minute sighting.

The object came to within a hundred feet of him and stopped. The UFO then began moving to John's left, making very slow, circular motions. John could still see the red glow from the bottom of the "massive ship." Then without warning, the object projected a thin red beam of light John says looked like a laser beam. This laser came from the underside of the object and shot into the water below. The object shut off the beam, moved to another location, and repeated this behavior. After several minutes of this "beaming" behavior, the UFO moved quickly back to the center of the reservoir, where it hovered. The object floated silently for not even half a minute, when all of its lights went out. Then, the object emitted a blinding burst of white light that seemed to be directed at John, knocking him to the ground. The next thing he remembers is getting up from the ground—but it was no longer dark. When he got to his feet, John noticed it was daylight. Sure enough, his watch told him it was just after eight o'clock in the morning. John is sure that the entire sighting was only twenty or so minutes long, yet he lost consciousness for several hours after being hit by the UFO's light beam. John's wife told me that during the next couple of days, her husband seemed distant and disoriented. It's my opinion that John had a contact experience, but to what extent, I'm not sure; John himself would rather forget about the entire incident than find out what happened during those missing hours.

### A Lake Encounter

This next lake encounter took place over Putnam Lake in Brewster, New York. The witnesses were two young women, Kris and Sue, both in their early thirties at the time. Once again, the sighting happened during the nighttime hours. The best way to present this case is to let you read the sighting account as told to me by Sue herself, an area resident.

#### Sue's Story

"Kris and I were returning home from work; we often carpool to save gas since we both live fairly close to each other in the Brewster-Patterson area. On July 12, 1987, we were driving down Fairfield Drive—off to the right is Putnam Lake. Just above the lake was a bright circle of pure white lights. The circle was high above the lake, just sitting there in the sky. I called out to Kris and said, 'Look at that!' She said that it was probably a blimp. I said there was no way this thing was a blimp since I had seen blimps in the area before—this looked nothing like them. I slowed down and watched the lights come down from the sky toward the northern part of the lake. I pulled onto Lake Shore Drive (which follows the lake more closely) and parked on the side of the road to get a better look at the lights. The time was about 11:30 PM. We got out of the car and walked to the shoreline, only about fifty feet from the road. The area is a pretty lonely place and we were a little scared to get out of the car.

"The UFO—and I say 'UFO' because we didn't know what it was—moved across the water no more than twenty feet above the lake. There seemed to be some sort of heat screen or shield extending down into the water, coming out from under this thing. Then, the UFO projected a beam of light into the water and the lights began vibrating. I heard a buzzing sound and could make out a sort of shape: it was triangular, like a pyramid. The UFO started vibrating faster and the buzzing got louder and louder; it got so loud we had to cover our ears. Without warning, the lights on the object went out and the whole thing just vanished. Kris and I were very excited—we knew that we had just seen a real UFO! We got back to the car and drove to the state police station on Route 22 in Brewster. We told the officer on duty what we saw and he looked at us and said, 'UFOs are not under our jurisdiction. You have to call NASA or the air force.' He even asked us if we'd been drinking. I was pretty insulted and the trooper said 'Oh, you must have seen those guys flying ultralight aircraft out of Stormville Airport, they always try to fake a UFO,' and he laughed. We left feeling very foolish and angry, and decided not to tell anyone else about our sighting."

### A 2007 Reservoir Sighting

This is a recent sighting over the West Branch Reservoir in Carmel, New York. The UFO was witnessed by multiple individuals and happened on July 19. Information about this event was emailed to me after I was featured on a radio show. Although there were a total of fourteen witnesses to this event, I was only able to speak with five of them. Three of them were unrelated, independent witnesses, and despite slight variations in perception, they all told basically the same story.

The sighting took place over the West Branch Reservoir causeway, an open bridge that follows Route 301. Driving across it any time of day or year is a beautiful, scenic experience. It is at this location, back in 1984, that dozens of people lined up at night in hopes of getting a glimpse of the Hudson Valley UFO. Those who did have sightings report the experience as life-changing and something that changed their views of reality. On a clear summer night in 2007, several residents were crossing the causeway in their cars, when the lead driver spotted something in the sky and slowed down. It wasn't long until the drivers behind him also saw it, and all the vehicles stopped on the road. The drivers and passengers got out and saw a series of white lights in a circular pattern in the northern sky, quite a fair distance from them. The simple fact that the lights were seen from so far away would indicate that it was one *very* large object, or ten or more different aircraft. There was no accompanying sound, and the object continued to approach where the witnesses were standing, all the while sinking in the sky. After a moment, the light circle was directly over the reservoir. The people who saw it knew something strange was going on because the lights seemed to be attached to one solid, very dark, triangular object. The UFO's size was estimated to be at least a hundred feet from apex to rear, and people could see a red light underneath the object that pulsated from being barely visible to becoming so bright it reflected off the water. The object dropped in altitude, and a red beam of light projected down into the water. When this happened, traffic was backing up on both sides of the causeway, and there were a dozen or more people watching the UFO. The dark triangle hovered above the water for about a minute, then all the lights "blinked out," and it was gone. One of the witnesses made a report to the local police, who told him they already had reports of strange lights in the sky. The police didn't plan on investigating the lights because one person called in and said he was able to identify the lights as small aircraft flying in formation. Over the next two months, a similar UFO was seen over several small reservoirs in Putnam County exhibiting the same characteristics and behavior.

## Why Are They Interested in the Reservoirs?

Many witnesses and others who heard about the sightings thought the "ship" could be tampering with the water supply, given its affinity for the reservoirs. Some speculated the objects were extracting the hydrogen from the water for fusion reactor fuel. I disagree—my analysis shows that these UFOs may have been interested in something entirely different.

In all 124 cases, the objects chose artificial lakes and reservoirs; there were no low-altitude sightings over natural lakes. This information is quite interesting and indicates a possible emerging pattern. In every artificial lake and reservoir investigated, I found a compass deviation between .32 and .8 degrees, indicating the presence of a magnetic anomaly. The natural lakes showed only a maximum of .10 degrees deviation. It seemed that the UFOs were attracted to the manmade bodies of water and their anomalies, rather than naturally occurring lakes.

The reason for the stronger anomaly in the artificial bodies of water lies in its geological features. Most of the area has iron ore in its substrate composition—high-grade magnetite, to be exact. The natural lakes were formed during the last ice age, when glaciers carved out the rock below and made the basins that later filled with water from the melting ice sheets. However, the glaciers didn't expose all the iron ore—a thick layer of granite remained on top. Conversely, artificial lakes and reservoirs made during the twentieth century used modern machinery and blasting for their formation. As a result, they're much deeper and the iron ore is completely exposed, explaining why the magnetic anomalies are stronger over these bodies. Residents in that area of New York have always complained about excessive iron in their tap water, resulting in frequent clogging of water filters. For years, researchers have been trying to make a solid connection between these magnetic anomalies and UFOs, and I believe my research has made this connection. To speculate a little further, perhaps the triangles are not extraterrestrial, but come from another dimension parallel to our own. It might be that the magnetic anomalies over the reservoirs are enhanced to curve space and allow the strange aircraft to slide back to their own reality.

### Recent Reports

The National UFO Reporting Center received well over five hundred reports during the period from 2007 to 2008, many of which were sightings of the black triangles. From January 2008 to March 2009, I received fifty-three reports by email from the United States and Canada describing close encounters with a dark, triangle-shaped UFO. I've studied the behavior of these triangular objects, and have shown that when compared to their disc-shaped counterparts, whoever or whatever is controlling them is considerably more aggressive. The number of sightings is increasing, and I believe there must be a reason for this.

# THREE

# THE CONTACT PHENOMENON

As I mentioned previously, I have been investigating the UFO phenomenon for a very long time, and with each passing year, I've noticed that cases are becoming more complex and puzzling. It seems that with each question we're able to answer, twenty more are raised, baffling my logic and confusing my concept of reality. If this imbalance between questions and answers continues, we may never understand what the UFO phenomenon and the contact experience represent. Drawing from my research and personal experiences, there is no doubt in my mind that UFOs are real. Evidence also indicates the intelligence behind contact phenomena has established communication with thousands of individuals on our tiny planet. As you might expect, there's no simple explanation for these events, and the intelligence seems to have multiple origins. I have seen enough evidence in my own investigations and the work of others to convince me that there isn't just one alien race interested in our planet. Who or what the intelligence is, and where they may be from, are more questions that need answers.

Although theories abound, not one investigator, researcher, or contactee can provide enough evidence to validate the UFO phenomenon's origin. Some people who claim to have had a contact experience "channel" information and actually preach to groups about the "true nature of the universe."[1] Well, no two stories of these contacts are the same, and if you get a number of these contactees in a room and let them talk for a while, they start arguing about who is correct and has "the truth." In my observation, people who channel angels, aliens, and spiritual masters have very little information about who or what they are in contact with but seem to delight in the belief of being specially selected, making them feel privileged and important.

In my early years of UFO research, I was satisfied to accept the idea that the bulk of the unknown UFO cases could be simply explained by the fact that the objects were nuts-and-bolts alien spaceships from other star systems. Today, I believe evidence indicates that in many cases, we are not dealing with a physical phenomenon, per se. It is my belief that many UFO sightings and claims of contact are the product of psychic (and on occasion, physical) communication with an incorporeal life form. These life forms can appear physical to us if they desire, and all seem to have the ability to shapeshift into different forms. It also seems that they have little difficulty assuming control over our minds and the way we perceive them. The UFO phenomenon is so varied that it just can't be explained easily as visitors in fan-

---

1 According to research from my files, covering 1977 to the present.

tastic spaceships from other star systems. I believe the truth is much more complex, and I'd be somewhat disappointed if the entire UFO experience—from the basic report of a close encounter of the first kind, to claims of being abducted by "aliens"—turned out to be nothing more than another race's explorers visiting our tiny planet, investigating life on our world.

Many claims of contact are more psychic rather than physical in nature, the reason for which I believe to be that we don't actually perceive the total sum of the phenomena. UFO intelligence may exist in four or more dimensions, and we, as three-dimensional beings with our limited senses, can't see into parallel realities. Where do these extra dimensions exist? Modern theoretical physics tells us the entire universe is layered in multiple dimensions and that at least one of these dimensions may be close to our own and exist in the same space, but at a right angle to a right angle, a direction in space we can't turn to see. If human beings could actually see in this direction, we would be able to perceive at least part of the multidimensional universe. Under normal circumstances, human beings can't see into this hidden dimension, and unfortunately, we may never be able to understand the true nature of UFOs or any other paranormal phenomena. Alien intelligence, therefore, can continue to interact and hide from us without our ever obtaining much information about them. There are several reasons why alien intelligence may prefer to stay hidden from humanity; the first of which being that they may have a limited-contact law forbidding the contamination of other civilizations, thereby interfering with their natural social and technological development. Another reason might be that they want to remain unseen because they're using us for their own purposes, only to their benefit. If they are experimenting with us on physical and psychic levels and abducting or controlling people against their will, you might understand why they would want to remain invisible.

An ancient Arabic tale tells of a race of beings that have the ability to shapeshift and control the minds of men and women. According to legend, they are said to live in a world that borders our own, and while they are able to perceive us, we can't see them. For thousands of years, the people of the Middle East have called this race of beings the *djinn*, which translates into English as "hidden."[2]

Since answers relating to the contact/UFO experience remain hidden from us, much mysticism and religion has been built up around it. History has shown us that when human beings do not understand something, they tend to attribute a supernatural cause to it. It's common today to hear people say that demons and ghosts are responsible for the manifestations we call UFOs. We must remember that whoever or whatever we're dealing with is an intelligent race of beings that exist in the multiverse alongside us. Since they aren't human and their technology seems "magical" to us, we must not attach pseudo-religious labels to them. The erroneous act of attaching worship (and the usual associated desire of our subservience) alters the way we perceive them and also

---

2 *Djinn* (or *jinn*, singular *jinni*) are Islamic devils or demons that existed on Earth before man. In the West, we call them "genies."

has a tendency to generate fear and paranoia. Throughout history, humans have feared things they didn't understand, a serious potential problem if and when first contact takes place on a global scale.

## Classifying Contact Experiences

UFO encounters can be classified into two main categories. The first is a sighting of a UFO, meaning when a person sees something unexplainable in the sky. In most cases of this type, the sighting is the only paranormal incident in the person's entire life, the sighting itself the result of co-incidence. Usually, the witness is with one other person or a group of people and their reports are mostly consistent, with only slight variations.

Before I talk about the second type of encounter—close en-counters—let me say first that I believe every close encounter is purposeful, not accidental. My analysis has me convinced that many cases of this type are types of a pre-contact experi-ence. At times, the contact may be so subtle that the person involved may not immediately identify it as such. Although not everyone who has a close encounter claims communica-tion with an alien intelligence, a considerable number of wit-nesses report feeling a connection that leads to various types of contact with nonhuman intelligence.

At first, when contactees talk about this kind of experi-ence to friends or an investigator, they usually only mention the sighting, and not the contact experience. Most are afraid to relate the more personal aspects of the experience, and have an easier time attributing events to their imaginations getting the best of them. In some close encounters, witnesses report feeling psychically "probed," and can sense the intelligence controlling the UFO. After investigating many claims of this nature, I believe the probing is some type of telepathic communication attempt during the sighting. In close encounters, a contact experience may take place in which the witness is abducted or an alien being appears and attempts communication. The attempt may happen during the encounter, hours or days later, or sometimes many years after the experience. In some case studies, a subtle initial contact is made after a close encounter sighting after which the witness may lead a normal life for many years. Then, without warning, the person wakes up one night in bed (or somewhere else) to find an alien creature standing over them while they lie immobilized on their bed or a strange, laboratory-type table.

Since these experiences are complex, it's sometimes very difficult to understand what type of contact the person is experiencing. I have placed the contact aspect of the UFO experience into five sub-categories; they are presented below with brief explanations and examples from my files.

## I: Close Encounter of the Third Kind

Abbreviated as CEIII, this is an experience in which people claim to have encountered some type of alien being near a grounded UFO. In some cases of this type, the "alien" may appear human, but most describe the being as humanoid, though definitely nonhuman. Most encounters of this type involve a sighting and the landing of an anomalous object with a humanoid creature close by. However, in rare cases, the UFO is seen in the sky but not on the ground, and the creatures are still reported in the vicinity. In just about every experience of this type, the humanoid being is associated with the sighting of an unknown object. Usually the creature looks at the witness, but no real conscious communication is made. In a large percentage of the cases, the witness later has another contact experience in which he or she is abducted or receives some type of detailed information by telepathic means.

### A Classic Close Encounter of the Third Kind

One of the first well-documented CEIII cases took place in the sixties and created quite a nationwide stir due to its involvement of a police officer who had an excellent service record. Dr. J. Allen Hynek personally investigated this case; at that time, he was the scientific consultant for Project Blue Book.[3] During one of our many get-togethers I asked him about this particular case. What is presented below are the notes taken during my conversation with him regarding this close encounter. Before he began relating the case, Dr. Hynek said this sighting was one of the "straws that broke the camel's back," so to speak, to make him believe in the

---

3 Project Blue Book was one of a series of systematic studies of UFOs conducted by the United States Air Force. Starting in 1952, it was the second revival of such a study. A termination order was given for the project in December 1969, and all activity under its auspices ceased in January 1970.

reality of the UFO phenomenon and convince him of their possible extraterrestrial origin.

The encounter began at 5:45 PM on April 24, 1964, in Socorro, New Mexico. Thirty-one-year-old policeman Lonnie Zamora was on patrol, when he was passed by an obviously speeding car. Zamora took off in pursuit, when he suddenly heard an explosion in the distance and saw an orange flame rising into the air. Officer Zamora knew of a dynamite shack in the direction of the conflagration, so he gave up chasing the speeder and instead headed in the direction of the dynamite shack, his assumption being that it had exploded. On his way to the site, he radioed the sheriff's office to inform them of what had taken place, and that he was en route to investigate. As Zamora proceeded toward the dynamite shack's area, he noticed rising smoke, which he thought was the aftermath of the explosion. He turned down a secondary narrow gravel road that wound around a small gully. As he approached the shack's location, he noticed a shining object approximately a hundred and fifty yards in the distance. His first reaction to this sight was that it was an overturned automobile, the gas tank exploded. But as he got closer, Zamora realized he was looking at an oval-shaped object lacking windows and doors, seemingly standing on several tripod-like legs extending from the object's sides or underside. He stated that the object was about the same size as a car, and he couldn't tell which end was the front or back. He noticed an unusual red insignia on the side of the object, and saw two small beings nearby. At first he thought they were children dressed in white overalls. He recalled that one of the beings jumped backwards when it noticed him, as if frightened. After overcoming the initial shock of what he was seeing, Zamora radioed the sheriff's office and explained the details of the incident as best he could. After finishing his report, he decided to get a closer look but was surprised by a loud roar and a bluish flame that shot out of the object's underside. He could no longer see the two little beings. Fearing that the object was going to explode, officer Zamora fell to the ground to protect himself. The object lifted into the air, and headed southeast, flying in a straight line. Having intercepted Zamora's earlier radio transmission, state police sergeant Sam Chavez arrived at the scene just after the craft disappeared into the sky. As other officers and investigators arrived, they discovered deep landing marks and footprints on the ground. FBI and air force personnel soon joined local authorities, and found bent and burned brush in several places surrounding the spot where the object had sat. Measurements taken by police verified that there were four indentations on the ground; the distance between them formed a quadrilateral whose diagonals intersected at exactly ninety-degree angles. Officer Zamora described the event in detail to all who reviewed the case and impressed even the most skeptical investigators. Dr. Hynek was also very impressed with Zamora's report and as he later recounted to me, puffing on his pipe in my living room, he noted that it was too bad the officer was the only witness, and that he didn't have a camera in his patrol car. Dr. Hynek also told me that the CIA was very interested in the Zamora sighting; agents paid the Socorro sheriff's office a number of visits to gather information. Dr. Hynek also said that later he discovered that except for local police officers, CIA agents were the first to arrive on the scene; they placed stones around the impressions in the ground to mark the positions of the object's landing legs. During Dr. Hynek's investigation of the Zamora incident, he requested that the CIA forward to him any information or documents they had regarding the Zamora case, but was denied.

## ALIENS AT CANDLELIGHT AIRPORT

In the mid-eighties, I had the privilege of investigating a close encounter of the third kind in my area. The encounter was at the tail end of the Hudson Valley UFO flap, so my name and contact information were easy to find, as local papers and radio stations often carried stories on the UFO sightings and my research. The witness was a forty-one-year-old business man who was driving home to New Milford, Connecticut, on Route 37 near Sherman. It was December 23, 1985, and the time was close to 8:30 PM. The man said he looked up to the sky and noticed a large object that was "lit up like a Christmas tree"—multicolored lights seemed to be attached to a solid structure that was shaped like a triangle. At first, he thought it was a large jet having trouble, making an emergency landing at the nearby Candlelight Airport. He knew this wasn't a good idea because the airport is a small airfield for private planes.

The object was completely silent, and the man was perplexed at how an aircraft of its size could move at such a low altitude without making any noise whatsoever. The witness continued to drive but lost the object behind the hills and the tree line. He made a right turn down Candlelight Road in New Milford and proceeded to the airport to get a better view of the large aircraft that was surely going to attempt landing in the field. As he slowly drove down the road, he noticed two cars pulled alongside the street with their emergency flashers on. The man stopped his car and was greeted by a man and a woman who said they had also seen the object, and followed it to this location. They pointed to the woods on the right and said they thought the aircraft landed in the trees. Sure enough, the woods seemed illuminated, as if something was there with its lights on. Thinking it was a downed aircraft, he said he would go investigate, and instructed the woman to find a house nearby and call the police. The other man volunteered to stay by the cars.

The man went back to his car, grabbed a flashlight, and proceeded to walk in the woods towards the lighted area. After walking for about a half mile or so, he saw what he described as a triangle-shaped aircraft hovering motionless just above the tree line. The object was dark except for one amber light on the bottom, illuminating the ground below. "It wasn't a beam of light . . . just a light that was bright enough to light up the ground," he said. The object was about sixty feet in the air and was at least seventy feet long. At times, the object seemed to sway slightly back and forth, making the trees below it move too. The man realized this wasn't any conventional type of aircraft, and he knew it was a UFO—perhaps the same object that everyone had been seeing in the area for the past seven years. Walking slowly and carefully through the woods towards the object, the man noticed three tall "men" standing motionless. "They were dark figures, very scary," he said. "I froze in my tracks and shut off my light." As he stood frozen with fear, one of the three figures started to walk in his direction. The man turned around and ran back towards the road, tripping on a number of thorn bushes. He was able to get up and keep running, never once looking back. When he finally reached the road, the police were just pulling up and there were at least five other cars along the shoulder. An officer asked him what was going on, so he told them about the object in the woods over the trees, but didn't mention the beings. The single patrolman called for backup and walked into the woods to investigate. After about fifteen minutes, another police cruiser pulled up as the officer returned from the woods, saying he didn't find anything.

## THE CREATURE WITH THE GLOWING EYES

More recently, several people who live in the Milford area have come forth with reports of a creature that seemed to be dressed in a dark tan one-piece suit. The creature was described as being at least seven feet tall with glowing, yellow eyes. The creature has been observed in the woods and crossing back roads at night. One report that came to my attention was from a family who own property in that area. They said the creature was observed on two occasions walking towards their home, and then vanishing like a ghost before it reached the porch. In the summer of 2009, I received an email from an area resident who apparently had a sighting of the same creature four years before the UFO sighting. Below is his statement as given to me via email.

I must make it very clear that this person had no idea of the content of this book or *Contact of the Fifth Kind*. In my opinion, his report provides more evidence of the creature's existence.

"In 1981, sometime in the summer, I had an experience at about 11:15 PM, while driving on the airport road. I was on my way home when I saw something that looked like a naked woman on the road. As I neared it, my headlights shined right into its eyes, making them reflect and glow with a gold color, like a cat's eyes. As I got closer, it was apparent the figure was not naked, but was wearing a tight-fitting suit that was light beige, almost the color of pale skin. Its hands were large and there were few strands of hair on its head. It stood there in the road like it was waiting for me. All I remember from that point on is that after my car passed it, everything went black. The next thing I knew, I was at the end of the airport road in the car and my hands were shaking. I made it home and went straight to bed. The next day, I took a shower and kept saying to myself that I had seen a ghost. Can you help me figure out what happened that night?"

It's apparent that more took place than the young man could remember; he experienced a certain amount of missing time. What took place during his "blackout"? Was he taken by some alien intelligence, or did he simply pass out after experiencing something terrifying? All of the sightings of this creature have been at night. Were they related to the encounter of the third kind near Candlelight Airport Road? I believe so, because my research shows various types of paranormal phenomena appearing right before and right after a UFO sighting, including sightings of bizarre creatures that do not seem to be part of our reality.

## II: A Close Encounter with a Telepathic Connection

In most UFO encounters, the witness observes an unidentifiable object, but no apparent contact is established. In some cases, however, the witness feels some type of psychic link with the UFO. The UFO seems to respond to the witness's emotions, and in rare cases, an actual thought or image is placed in the person's mind—a telepathic message, so to speak, from the intelligence inside the UFO.

### The May 27, 1988, Connecticut Encounter

On May 27 at approximately 9:30 PM, a giant triangle-shaped UFO appeared over the skies of Newtown, Connecticut, very close to the I-84 corridor. The UFO was reported to have flown over the homes of at least two hundred residents. Witnesses reported the object as much larger than conventional aircraft, flying very low in the sky. Some people said that a multicolored beam of light came out of the underside of the object and engulfed a number of homes in the area. All witnesses agree that the object had a semicircle or boomerang pattern of lights on the front, attached to a dark triangular object. At least twenty lights were reported, in all sorts of colors: red, blue, green, white, and yellow or amber. For the most part, the object made no sound, although some people said they heard a faint humming sound, like a finely tuned electric motor as it passed directly overhead. All agree that the UFO was very large, perhaps two to three hundred feet from end to end. As the object made its pass over the cities of Waterbury, Newtown, Danbury, and Southbury, it would occasionally stop for a short period of time—almost as if it had found what it was looking for. It was at these times a beam of light would appear from under the dark triangle and project to the ground. The interesting part of this sighting is that out of the fifteen people who claimed to have been engulfed in the beam of light, thirteen said they saw images of alien-looking beings or had a vision of a room in which strange-looking people were working on humans strapped to black tables. According to a number of the people who experienced the vision phenomenon, the aliens looked like tall men with slanted yellow eyes and leathery skin. The vision caused considerable fear in the people who experienced it; some of them interpreted the vision as meaning they were next. Two out of the fifteen people didn't see any type of vision, but claimed to have felt a connection with the object in the sky—they could "feel" what the intelligence was thinking. One person claimed to have heard a voice say, "We have come from a faraway place and you have been selected to take part. We do not want to frighten you, but will do what we have to." After causing quite a ruckus for about an hour, the giant UFO departed somehow, and wasn't reported in any surrounding areas. In the entire collection of witness reports, not one person saw the object move away, or even vanish in the sky. There were also no reports from any of the neighboring states, including New York, Massachusetts, and Rhode Island. If this was a physical craft, where would it be practically hidden? When not being seen in the sky (and given that the dark triangles are mostly seen at night), where could you possibly park something that huge during the day?

Two days later, the same UFO was spotted again. Although contact in the next case is not as apparent as the encounters above, I believe it occurred nevertheless. UFO researchers and paranormal investigators have to carefully analyze reports of witnesses who experience a contact-type close encounter because the contact itself is not always obvious. Sometimes it is not presented to the researcher at all during the interview because the witness wants to be believed and may consider information of alien contact too fantastic or personal to tell someone they've only just met. Therefore, it's important to not push a witnesses for information, especially during the first interview. If an investigator feels there was more to the sighting, he or she should schedule another session in the near future.

The sightings on both dates mentioned earlier were verified by Connecticut state police—at least one trooper going east on I-84 saw the object. When questioned by local media, a spokesperson for the state police said they had received many calls about a strange object in the sky and that one officer did in fact see it while on patrol. The officer was not made available for comment, and police explained the sightings on both dates as being nothing more than a group of hang gliders flying in formation with "Chinese lanterns of different colors hanging from the bottom of their wings." One witness to the sighting on both dates called this explanation "the prattling of idiots."

The UFO that appeared over the skies of Connecticut in 1988 was no doubt under some kind of intelligent control, but who or what was this intelligence? Was it human, alien, or something even more fantastic? Once again, it appeared to survey the area by projecting a beam of light capable of engulfing homes, vehicles, and individuals. The UFO then returned to some of the houses it scanned at a later date, resulting in some form of contact with one or more of the people who lived there.

## III: A Close Encounter with Entity Communication

This form of contact is characterized by the individual claiming to have had verbal or telepathic communication with a human-like or nonhuman entity. In most cases, the person is left with some type of information, but in rare incidences, only a name or a few words are consciously remembered. Some of these encounters take place inside a ship, others do not. Numerous reports in my file tell of the entity appearing in the middle of the night, standing in front of the person's bed. This nighttime visitation usually takes place after a close encounter. However, I do have reports where contact of this nature took place without the witness having a previous UFO sighting or any other type of paranormal experience. To make matters even more complex, this type of contact is not restricted to the above—there are several cases in my files where the experiencer claims that on more than one occasion, an extraterrestrial entity "popped in" while the person was driving, and engaged the captive driver in a lengthy conversation.

In past accounts, I've tried to use witnesses' real names, but in this case the witness is referred to only as "Jane." At the time of the experience, Jane was thirty-five and lived with her husband and two young children in Mamaroneck, New York. When I first spoke with Jane she was still very upset about her experience, because something like this had never happened before in her entire life. Her story is presented below as told to me on June 23, 1992.

On June 20, at 11:00 PM, Jane was getting ready to retire for the night. Her husband was already in bed and the two children were fast asleep. As she walked into the bedroom, she looked up through the skylight in the room and saw a bright, star-like object right over the window. Jane thought its brightness was strange because of its intensity and the fact that she didn't remember seeing a star that bright in that position. She got into bed and soon fell asleep.

Several hours later, she was awakened by a strange buzzing sound. She opened her eyes to look at the time—it was 3:35 AM. She again looked toward the skylight and saw a beam of light project through the glass, illuminating the foot of the bed. The beam split into a number of colors, looking like a rainbow. The light then traveled up the bed until it was covering half her body, and although she had a sheet on, she could feel warmth from the light. Jane tried to move but realized she was paralyzed, and could only move her head. She looked over at her husband and noticed he was on his back, a position that he never sleeps in. His eyes and mouth were open as if he were dead, but she was relieved to see he was still breathing. "He looked like he was in a trance," she said.

After another two or so minutes, another beam of light came through the skylight. This time, the beam was white and a figure began to materialize inside the glow. The light shut off and she saw a very tall man standing at the foot of her bed. She told me, "He was at least seven feet tall, dressed in blue robes. He had long black hair and his skin looked very pale." The being just stood there and stared at Jane; she could do nothing but just lie there, paralyzed. The being then raised his hand, pointed to her, and told her out loud that her husband had not been harmed in any way. The being then said she would soon be receiving messages that would help the human race through the very hard times approaching in the future. Jane blacked out. When she woke up the next day, she told her husband about the experience. He laughed and told her it must have been a dream.

Since the experience, while asleep at night, Jane claims to be receiving some type of communication with the same being. At present, the messages consist of teachings and predictions of major events that will affect the human race in the years after 2010. One of these predictions was of a major hurricane hitting the East Coast in the late summer of the near future. I believe Jane's story; she is not looking for publicity and has nothing to gain by reporting her experiences. Since the initial contact, Jane has acquired a large following of people who come to hear her sing. Jane never took a voice lesson in her life, but is now able to sing with the voice of an angel. The lyrics in the songs are spiritual teachings of happiness and hope. She will admit to only a few that the songs are channeled from the "angelic realm"; most of the people who attend her sessions have no idea of their origin. Jane does not charge for the sessions, and unlike most people who channel, she doesn't preach and insist that everyone believe her. The entity that channels the songs through Jane is called Isliam and claims to be from another "plane of existence in a galaxy two hundred million light years from Earth." Jane is one of many credible people who have had their lives changed by the contact experience. Although I suspect that this Isliam entity is hiding its true identity, the results of the contact and the effect it's had on the many who attend the sessions are positive in nature. Perhaps there's a very subtle extra and/or ultraterrestrial plan in the works to slowly change the consciousness of the human race on this planet using not only channeled teachings and images, but also music.

## A SIMILAR NIGHTTIME VISIT

One of the advantages of being a published author is that you get a great deal of mail (both positive and negative) in response to your work, but the best part by far is receiving new cases to expand your personal file library. In the mid-nineties, I received a letter from a woman named Sally in her mid-thirties, living just outside of Houston, Texas. This woman had an experience similar to Jane in New York. Sally was awakened at about 3 AM to find a tall man standing by her bed. She described the man as "Egyptian looking," with long, black hair and very pale skin. Although the room was dark, the being seemed to glow and she could clearly make out his facial features. Sally told me in her letter:

"He was just standing there looking at me; I was so scared that I could not move. My husband was sleeping right next to me and this was strange, usually he is a very light sleeper, but no matter what I did, I could not wake him up. He was snoring very loudly, and I'd never heard him snore before. This man was just looking at me and his eyes were very dark with a red area that glowed in the middle of his pupils. He then raised his finger and he pointed to the ceiling and just vanished like he was being beamed aboard a ship, like in *Star Trek*. I was so scared but for some reason, I couldn't scream. I pulled the covers over my head and then heard a voice say, 'You will now travel far beyond any place you have ever been before.' I then felt as if I was falling into a hole, sinking, and then I blacked out. The next day when I woke up, I felt very tired, and my husband said I looked pale. I went to the doctor and he said I had developed an iron deficiency somehow."

Sally continued to have contact experiences into 2005 and claimed that she actually met the "aliens" face to face a number of times aboard their ship. She said, "They look like us, but can change their shape into a number of limited forms. They can't change into a car or a table, but they can alter their appearance to look human or like themselves." As of the publication of this book, I am no longer in contact with Sally. Her phone number has been disconnected and she seems to have vanished off the face of the Earth. Although this is not a common ending for most contactees, it happens occasionally.

In some cases, nighttime visitations from unknown intelligence doesn't take place in the bedroom; they take place outdoors. I would like to relate a very interesting phone call received from a middle-aged man who lives in Farmingdale, New York. A synopsis of the call is given below; I believe the individual had a contact experience with some type of inter-dimensional entity. The witness's name is on file but has been withheld here.

## A DIMENSIONAL PORTAL AND FIERY ENTITIES

"I have been living on and off in Saugerties, New York, for the past twenty years. During that time, I witnessed two un-usual happenings I thought might interest you. Although the experiences took place in 1989, I feel they'll be of some value to your research.

"I have a cabin on the Esopus River, a very narrow wa-terway that comes from the Ashokan Dam, leading to the Hudson River. I live just above the dam at Saugerties, and it is a very secluded and wooded area. I have the only prop-erty with a sandy beach, waterfront access, and it's about two hundred and fifty acres, so I really have no neighbors, to give you an idea of the isolation. I would also like to men-tion that my home is in a valley between two high moun-tains. The distance between the mountains is about three hundred feet across. I'm a pilot, and have landed my aircraft on this waterway many times. Now that you have some idea of the area, I can describe to you what took place. Also, I haven't told anyone about this happening to date.

"It was about three AM and I was asleep, when I was wo-ken by a humming noise. It sounded like I was in some type of generator room. I looked out the window but didn't see anything out of the ordinary. Looking down to the water-front, however, I saw a glow of light coming from my other home. I dressed and went to the water's edge. I looked up the river and noticed the glowing light was actually a large ball; as I watched, it slowly ascended to tree height, about a hundred feet or so from the ground. This ball of light was about half the size of my three-room cottage and it just hovered for about ten seconds. It then moved upward and beyond my line of sight. The night was rather foggy, which explains why the light glowed instead being sharply defined.

"The sighting was exciting, and I hoped I'd just witnessed a UFO. But after the excitement passed, I gave way to common sense, attributing the incident to some freak light distortion from the nearby highway. As I turned to go back into the house, I noticed some small lights in the trees just a few hundred yards away from the house, down a path in a heavily wooded area. The lights seemed strange, like fireflies in the summer. It was late October, too cold for fireflies to be out. I started to walk toward the lights and noticed that there were hundreds of them all over the ground. They seemed to glow like embers in a fireplace. These 'embers' looked like they were dancing in the air and avoiding each other like they were alive.

"I bent over for a closer look, when I felt heat in the area. It was like entering a heated room—a blast of warm, dry heat that made me feel very relaxed. There was enough heat to make me sweat, and I also realized that the closer I got to the lights, the warmer it felt, making me more tired and exhausted. It was as if all my energy was being drained. Since I was at the cabin alone, I decided not to stay and investigate any longer; I just couldn't fight the feeling of exhaustion. I also recall that the heat was not only around me, but also coming down from above. The heat was far stronger from above me than what I felt close to the ground. I looked up to see what could be causing the heat, but only saw an area of about thirty feet that looked like a distorted field. I thought that this might be some type of infrared radiation area, but from where, I couldn't tell. It seemed as if the heat was up there appearing out of nowhere.

"Now, I know the laws of physics, and one basic law states that energy cannot be destroyed or created out of nothing, it has to be changed or channeled from somewhere else. Well, wherever this energy was coming from was invisible. I looked up and felt the heat blasting against my face as if there was a heater up there! It was a very strange experience to feel this yet see nothing. For a moment, I wanted to do nothing but stand there in that good feeling. I mentioned earlier that I felt drained of energy, but the heat did feel good and seemed to relax me the more I stood there. Then, for no apparent reason, I found myself walking back to the house. I don't even remember deciding to leave, turning around, or anything. I *do* remember feeling very good while walking, like my spirit was ecstatic for no apparent reason. I reached my house and went to bed. I glanced at the clock—it said six AM. This was strange because I knew I couldn't have been out for more than thirty minutes, yet here was about two hours of time that couldn't be accounted for.

"The sleep I experienced was the most peaceful I'd had in my life, and when I woke up the next morning, I went back to where I saw the light and "embers" to see if there was any evidence, but found nothing. I still felt very good and didn't give any thought as to what took place until that evening. The more I thought about the previous night's events, the more confused I became. It was a silly feeling trying to piece the puzzle together. Every time I tried to recount the experience, the less clear it became, and so I thought I'd better write it down—it was fading very quickly. I read an article you (Phil Imbrogno) wrote in a magazine, and when I read it, it was like recalling a dream.

"Ever since having my experience, I feel that I'm not alone, that someone is with me all the time. Sometimes I get thoughts in my head and I find myself explaining things, like how I feel when I drink a beer when I'm thirsty . . . stupid things like that, but I have no control over it. There have been times where a multitude of thoughts would pass through my mind and then fade away. These thoughts don't even seem like my own. Since the incident, I've started to recall some other strange things that happened to me in the past, things I'd forgot about.

"One very important incident occurred on June 14, 1988. I was flying my aircraft from Massachusetts to Long Island, along the Long Island south shoreline. At the Jones Beach Tower, the aircraft engine lost power. I was about five hundred feet above ground level, over the water. Experts would tell you I had twenty-six seconds to land or I'd crash. As I turned the aircraft, I saw what appeared to be a silver light in the sky. I was worried about my situation and knew I couldn't make all the critical decisions. Then, all of a sudden, a multitude of ideas flashed in my head, and I was able to make all the necessary control adjustments in a very short amount of time. I knew exactly what to do with every control and landed perfectly. Thinking back, this would have been impossible because I could have never done this before; even an expert, super-experienced pilot would have trouble making these corrections to the aircraft which, again, had no engine power. It seemed that in that moment, I had an ability to decipher information very quickly."

In my opinion, the above person had a contact experience. During the two hours or so of missing time, it seems information was programmed into his mind from some unknown intelligence. The "heat" he experienced could have been an energy surge from an interdimensional source, rather than from an invisible ship. The firefly effect is interesting because in areas where UFOs are seen (areas of magnetic anomalies), these so-called "fireflies" are a common sight. Centuries ago, they were associated with fairies and otherdimensional earth spirits. I don't necessarily believe they were the intelligence responsible for the man's experience, but they could be a byproduct of the opening of a dimensional window, a portal opened by some type of intelligence to establish a link between themselves and humanity. This witness may have had contact experiences going as far back as childhood. He recalls a number of childhood events where he would see strange figures in his room, but the figures never tried to communicate with him.

### IV: A Close Encounter with Alien Abduction

Stories of human beings being abducted by aliens are common themes in a paranormal television shows and movies. Abductees are those who claim to have been taken aboard a UFO, usually against their will, with some kind of interaction with the alien intelligence operating the craft. This type of contact case is often referred to as a Close Encounter of the Fourth Kind. In most cases of this type, witnesses report medical procedures of some type being performed on them, with very little interaction otherwise. In some cases, no medical or other type of procedure is done. Instead, the person is shown incredible feats of technology such as three-dimensional navigational renderings or other complex devices, and is given information about the universe and its inhabitants.

## Contact and a Possible Family Abduction

Mr. Paul Dummas lives in Southbury, Connecticut, and had a very interesting experience resulting from the May 27, 1988, Connecticut sightings. I interviewed him and his family members at the 1988 Omega UFO Conference. Mr. Dummas said the UFO passed right over his home at 9:30 PM, whereupon he called his family to come out and see the approaching object. The Dummas family ran out to the back porch just in time to see the object pass directly overhead. Mr. Dummas said the UFO was so huge that when they looked up, it blocked out the entire sky—all they could see was a large mass drifting noiselessly above them.

"The object was so enormous that it took forever to pass over. It was no more than a thousand feet up and must have been at least two football fields long, moving at a very slow speed." Mr. Dummas paused here while recounting his sighting and said to me, "You're not going to believe this, but later that night, a smaller UFO came back to my home at about three in the morning. For some reason, I woke up and ran to the window to see an object approaching. It looked like a black . . . thing behind a white cloud, and it was moving closer and closer to my house. Then all of a sudden, I found myself back in bed, thinking it was all a dream. My wife was also awake and told me she had a strange dream about seeing a bunch of little guys in a spaceship. I went to the bedroom of my two sons, turned on the light, and found them both asleep. I was shocked to see their pillows smeared with blood from their nose. I woke them both up and then my six-year-old daughter came into the bedroom yelling out, 'Are they gone?!' I asked her who she meant and she replied, 'The spacemen who came through the walls to take us away!'"

It seems that the daughter had a conscious recollection of being abducted by small aliens she said resembled "monster men."

Mr. Dummas was quite upset about the entire incident; he heard speakers at the UFO conference talk about abductions and implants placed in a person's nasal cavity, amongst other types of procedures. I calmed him down and assured him that his experience didn't necessarily mean his family was abducted by aliens. I told him that sometimes there are logical explanations for these kinds of events. Mr. Dummas had brought his entire family to the conference to look for answers and speak with people who are experienced in investigating UFOs, but all he found was more fear and paranoia, increasing his trauma.

As of the writing of this book, Mr. Dummas hasn't had any more experiences with a UFO or aliens, but his daughter, now in her mid- to late twenties, continues to have an interest in the subject. She has since had several more UFO sightings and contact with an alien intelligence that continues to the present day. I am working with her and, in the near future, will have more information on a case I believe will prove fascinating to my fellow researchers and readers.

## CONTACT AND A FEAR OF THE NIGHT

On May 29, 1988, the triangle-shaped UFO was seen once again crossing a highway at a low altitude, but this time it was heading northwest. At that time, an interesting close encounter took place in the small Connecticut town of New Milford, about ten miles north of I-84. At about 10 PM, a Mr. Robert Nellis, at the time a twenty-five-year-old area resident was parked in his car with his friend Jeff and his dog. They were in the northern area of New Milford on a side road off Route 7, listening to the radio. They had spent the day boating on the Connecticut River and were all exhausted.

Suddenly, the dog started barking and crying, so Jeff looked around for what could causing the agitation. To the northeast, he saw a number of lights hovering over some pine trees less than a quarter of a mile away. Without warning, the lights began moving toward them and the car radio began to sound funny, with all types of strange-sounding static that interfered with the station's reception.

Robert and Jeff continued to watch the lights move toward them, and as they drew closer, they were amazed at the object's size. In an interview, they told me the UFO was at least the size of a football field. Jeff's dog continued to bark as the object passed over their car. Robert looked up and saw a very dark structure connecting the lights extending towards the object's rear. He told me the UFO was actually tear-shaped rather than semicircular as they had originally guessed, due to the formation shape of the lights. As the object passed over, they reported that it was so huge that it blocked out the entire sky overhead.

"This UFO was made of some type of very dark material, giving off very little reflection. It didn't make any sound, and was no more than five hundred feet above the car," Robert said. After passing over their car, the UFO then shifted towards the north. Robert then added, "We both saw some type of flashing lights under the object that looked like strobe lights. One last thing—when the object left, the dog was quiet, but when we first saw the UFO, he was in the back of the car, barking up a frenzy. Now that the thing was gone, he was in the front with us. I don't remember him jumping to the front and because he's a German shepherd, I think I would have been aware of him doing that. I asked Jeff, and doesn't remember the dog moving up to the front seat either."

Both watched the UFO as it moved slowly northwest. The total duration of the sighting was only ten minutes, yet there was a forty-minute difference between the clock in the car and the clock when they got home. Stranger still, Jeff's wristwatch was also forty minutes behind, keeping the same time as the clock in the car. Robert called me for several weeks after the sighting, saying that since the encounter, he felt "uneasy, restless, and upset." He also said that he was afraid to go out at night and was even fearful about talking about his sighting because he knew "they" would be angry. When I asked him who "they" were, he replied, "I don't know who they are, but I know they can hear me and they know what I'm doing." I lost track of both Robert and Jeff as of 1990 and from what I could find out, both men moved somewhere out west.

## A Close Encounter of the Third Kind and a Double Abduction

In 1995, I received a call from an individual who lived in Putnam county who claimed to have had "a close encounter" where he saw "alien beings" with his girlfriend. I arranged to meet the man as soon as possible because experiences of this type must be investigated soon after they occur. This case was also important to me because it involved a form of contact that took place in the Hudson Valley area. Although the interview was several hours long, an edited version of the experience, including the important data, is presented here.

At the time, Shawn was a thirty-year-old construction worker and resident of Croton Falls, New York. Sally, his thirty-two-year-old girlfriend, was also from the same area. It was August 15, at about 2 AM, and they were driving to Mahopac on Route 6 after attending a friend's party in a nearby town. As they drove, they noticed a glow off the right side of the road that looked like a brush fire. They turned off Route 6 onto a small road and slowed the car down. Shawn says he felt driven—almost compelled—to check out the situation, but Sally had a bad feeling, and told Shawn they should just go to the police and report the incident. Shawn didn't seem to be paying attention to her, and said, "Look at that! It's like energy coming from the ground . . . we've *got* to check this out!" As he continued towards the "fire," he saw a number of flashing lights ahead blocking the road. At first he thought they were fire or police vehicles because the lights were blue and red. He stopped his car and saw two "small men" walking toward him. Thinking they were policemen, Shawn got out of his car and walked to meet the approaching figures. As the "men" drew closer, he noticed that they were much too short to be fire fighters or police officers, and thought they might be kids fooling around. As they moved out of the glare of the lights, he realized they weren't human at all! He described the creatures having large heads, long arms, and no hair. As they continued their approach, the lights of Shawn's car reflected in their eyes, glowing red.

Shawn ran back and got into his car and yelled to Sally to lock all the doors. He then told her to jump in the back seat and pull a blanket over herself to hide from whatever these things were. Somehow, he knew it was her they were after—not him. The beings came right up to the doors and the front windshield of the car. Shawn told me, "It was as if they didn't know how to work the handle on the car door. They kept on passing their hands over the front of the glass, expecting the door to open." He noticed there were three of them now, one on the right, one on the left, and one in front of the car. He described the beings as being less than five feet tall with large, pear-shaped heads. He described their eyes as being huge and curving around their heads. To him, they almost looked like the eyes of an insect.

*A typical "gray" alien*
*(Photo credit: author)*

The beings continued to try to enter the car, and then Shawn started hearing "voices" inside his head. He knew it was some type of communication attempt from these creatures.

"They tried to get me to open the door by convincing me that the lock is open in the 'down' position . . . it almost worked because I started to pull the lock up but stopped myself. Then I looked at the front windshield and it began to melt in front of my eyes! I closed my eyes, looked again, and the windshield was all right. I know they tried to scare me out of the car by putting images of danger in my mind. I also had thoughts that the car was on fire and ready to blow up. I tell you, these beings did all this to try to get me to open the car door so they could get us.

"I then knew that it was not me that they wanted . . . it was Sally, and they knew she was in the back of the car. What's strange is that I didn't hear her at all. You would think that with all this going on, she'd be screaming. It was as if she had fallen asleep under the blanket in the back. I yelled at the aliens to leave her alone because she already had a hysterectomy. I'm not sure why I said this, but somehow I knew what they wanted. Then I felt very light-headed and closed my eyes for a second. When I opened them, I was outside the car and Sally was nowhere in sight. I don't know how I left the car, but now there were six of those alien guys all around me in a circle. One came forward and I thought he said that they were going to let me go when they finished. I cried and yelled for them to let me go, but this guy was very emotionless. It was like it was his job and no matter what I did, he was going to do what he had to. I felt like some type of specimen and this was the Jacques Cousteau of outer space—he was going to capture and study me no matter how much I protested.

"The next thing I knew, the sun was rising and it was light out and we were back in the car, parked alongside the road. Sally was sitting in the front with me and all we did was stare at each other. We didn't talk too much about what happened; it was like both of us were in shock. About a week later, we broke up. She accused me of being in league with the aliens and said I purposely took her to the place where they were waiting so she could be experimented on. When I called her at her job, they told me they think she left the area, and I haven't seen her since."

I asked Shawn if the car was still running during the incident and if so, why didn't he just take off. He replied that he didn't even think about driving away because there were so many thoughts in his mind during the experience, it put him in a very confused state. He also said that after the encounter, he can't remember if the car was still running or not. Perhaps during the encounter, this unknown intelligence barraged Shawn with telepathic thoughts to keep him distracted so he couldn't make any decisions. It's also clear that Sally must have had more of a conscious recollection of the abduction. It's too bad she couldn't be reached and my attempts to track her down have also failed; she had no family in the New York area.

Shawn refused to undergo hypnosis or see one of the therapists I know who treats people experiencing post-traumatic, paranormal experiences. Many researchers believe that some type of genetic experiment is being conducted on humans by this alien intelligence. Was this the reason they were so interested in Sally? Shawn still lives in the area and has gone on with his life, convinced he was abducted by aliens that night. As of 2009, he hasn't had any more paranormal experiences.

## V: A Close Encounter with Channeling

The phenomenon of channeling refers to a particular type of contact wherein a person claims to be in mental contact with a nonhuman, human, or superhuman intelligence. Although most channelers claim to be psychic mediums, some do not. In rare cases, a channeler leads a fairly normal life until contact begins. The contact itself usually starts after a close encounter with a UFO or a nighttime visitation from an alien entity, but this is not always the case. Communication from the "aliens" is made orally, by automatic writing, or even through diagrams and art used to convey the entity's message. In channeling, the person is usually taken over by the intelligence, but not in all cases. The person who channels may or may not have had a UFO sighting, but most have a history of experiencing paranormal events since childhood. The great majority of the information conveyed during a channeling session seems to be pat philosophical statements about human nature that border on dogmatic. In rare cases, actual technical information is channeled, and a manifestation of some type of psychic, physical, or poltergeist phenomenon takes place during a session. These cases offer more data to study, but are few and far between. Although I have found that at least nine out of ten channelers are charlatans or people with overactive imaginations, there are a select few who have produced enough evidence to convince me that in rare cases, outside intelligence is involved. The two cases presented here involve contact with manifestations of psychic and physical phenomena, and have convinced me that some of us are indeed in communication with more than our imaginations.

## THE AMAZING CONTACTS OF J. DEAN FAGERSTROM

I first met Dean Fagerstrom in the summer of 1982 when he lived in the town of Putnam Lake. He was married, had two children, and claimed to be in contact with a number of extraterrestrial/spiritual entities using him to impart information into our world. Dean originally wrote Dr. J. Allen Hynek (mentioned in the beginning of this book) a letter in 1981 explaining his contact with a being known as

"Donestra" from a planet called "Solarian." Dr. Hynek was impressed with the letter—it was very well written and the author seemed to truly believe in the fantastic claims he was making. Dr. Hynek sent me copy of the letter and insisted I pay Mr. Fagerstrom a visit, since he was not far from my home.

It was the summer of 1982 when I first met Dean. In our initial interview, I found him to be intelligent, articulate, and one of the most fascinating individuals I have ever met in this area of study, to say the least. Dean was a wonderful host and was very cooperative when I encouraged him to talk about his contact experiences. There was no hesitation on Dean's part; he told his story and seemed to trust me with the information. Dean spoke with great ease, telling me all about his experiences like someone talking about their last vacation.

Although Dean's contacts seem to date back to his childhood, his adult experiences began in 1966 while he was in the army, stationed at Bad Kreuznach, Germany. Dean lived downtown, about a mile from the base. One night in November, at two o'clock in the morning, he was sitting in his apartment at a desk working on a number sequence to predict the lottery. Dean began to feel strange, as if someone was in the apartment watching him. He felt a presence strongly enough to make him get up and search the rooms. He describes the feeling as nonthreatening, but he was concerned nevertheless. After finding no one in any of the rooms, he returned to his desk and looked at the white board he was using to tape pages on. Suddenly, a human-like face appeared before his eyes! The face filled up just about the entire three-feet-square board. As the image got clearer, he saw that it was not one face, but two. There was a bluish shimmer around the edges of the image, and he could now make out the face of a man, and the other of a woman. The man had shoulder-length blonde hair while the woman had slightly darker and shorter hair. Both had what Dean described as "piercing blue eyes." Dean was somewhat surprised by this apparition, but, strangely, felt no fear. He looked at the faces and knew that he had seen them before; they seemed very familiar. Just then, he heard a voice close to his ear say the materializing beings' names. The male gave his name as "Donestra," and the female gave her name as "Kilestra," Donestra's wife.

Donestra told Dean he knew everything about him—he had been receiving his thought projections for years. Donestra said that the faces he was seeing weren't real; they were holographic projections. Donestra and Kilestra told Dean they were among thousands of other individuals from various planets throughout the near regions of the universe who have ascended to a higher plane of existence. Occasionally, ascended beings like them would interact with other life forms in the physical universe to help them achieve a higher state of consciousness. Donestra told Dean that they had been studying Earth for many years and that our planetary and human condition was of great interest to them.

After several minutes of conversation, the communication came to a close and Dean was asked to not mention what had taken place to anyone. The two beings told Dean to watch the skies in the next few days—he would be shown a sign confirming the communication was real and not a dream. A few days later, Dean felt drawn to a window and looked at the night sky where he saw a huge "starship" that performed amazing maneuvers. The sighting of this strange ship was what Dean was waiting for; it proved that the contact with Donestra was real and not some late-night hallucination.

A year later, Dean was discharged from the service and he moved to Brewster, a small New York city close to the Connecticut border. Things were quiet and the year went by uneventfully. Then on January 19, 1968, at 4:30 in the morning, Dean had another experience with an extraterrestrial intelligence, a contact encounter that changed his life.

He woke up that morning and saw a bluish shimmer in the upper corner of the room. He also heard a high-frequency buzzing sound that vibrated his head and made him feel uneasy. Gradually, an object about three inches in diameter materialized in the location of the blue light. The object was round and metallic-looking, and resembled an old-fashioned microphone.

This strange object started to move, and slowly approached Dean until it stopped no more than ten inches in front of his face. It floated there and continued to emit a sound that oscillated at a very high frequency. As Dean watched this device, something projected itself from the center of a disc and extended out four or five inches, in alignment with the top frontal part of his head. The projection resembled an ice pick and seemed to Dean to be some type of probe. The probe came to within three inches of his forehead and emitted a very intense vibration that shook his head and neck. Dean lay helpless in bed for several minutes until the device completed its task. The object then went quiet and vanished right before his eyes. Dean then fell into a deep sleep.

The next day, Dean felt compelled to go to an art store to buy graph paper, pencils, triangles, compasses, and other types of drafting instruments. The buying spree didn't seem to be under his control, nor did he understand why he was collecting these things. Dean took his purchases home and locked himself in his study, where for the next seventy-two hours, he drew various types of alien machinery. Dean had no idea why he was doing this, but knew that Donestra was somehow involved. He had very little idea what the devices were or what they were used for. Along with the diagrams, he produced a number of equations and symbols in an unknown language.

Dean didn't know what the completed drawing would look like, but felt strongly motivated to complete them anyway. The diagrams were created in a very unusual manner: he would place a piece of graph paper in front of him and stare at it. After several seconds, bluish dots would appear on the paper showing him where to connect lines. He seemed to have a pre-knowledge of what color or shade to place in a particular part of the diagram, and what to name each diagram, but overall, he received little technical information. After three days behind closed doors, and with very little food and water, Dean finished the last of the diagrams, thirty-two in total. Dean then put the diagrams in a notebook and filed them away; Donestra had told him that when the day came, he would know who to give them to, someone referred to as the "prime mover."

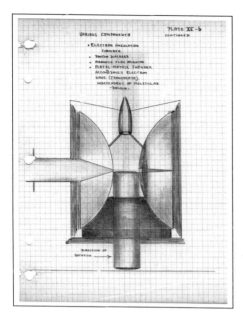

Device channeled through
Dean Fagerstrom by
Donestra
(Photo credit: author)

Device channeled through
Dean Fagerstrom by
Donestra 2
(Photo credit: author)

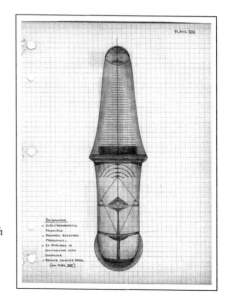

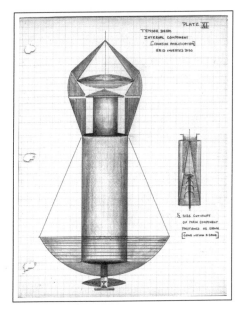

*Device channeled through Dean Fagerstrom by Donestra 3*
*(Photo credit: author)*

As the years passed, Dean continued his contact with Donestra, resulting in the writing of three unpublished five-hundred-page manuscripts: *The Book of Solarian, The Celestial Citizen,* and an untitled one. Although I was able to read all three, Dean's originals and my copies seem to have vanished. Dean said that one day while sitting outside with the manuscripts, he fell into a deep sleep and when he woke up about an hour later, the manuscripts were gone. I then looked for my copies in my library, but couldn't find them. This was incredibly strange because I had all my research material on the Fagerstrom case in one particular file cabinet. The diagrams were still there, as were other media, but the manuscripts were nowhere to be found. Perhaps Donestra changed his mind and decided the human race was not yet ready for the knowledge contained within the writings, or perhaps my copies were misplaced and Dean's originals just blew away with the wind—we may never know!

Once when speaking with Dean about the information he obtained from Donestra, something very weird happened. He stopped mid-sentence, went blank, and stood still for about forty-five seconds, as if in a trance. He spoke again and said, "He was here." "Who was here?" I asked. "Donestra was here," he said. "He instructed me to turn the diagrams over to you. He said you will know what to do with them when the time comes." Dean completed the diagrams back in 1968 and held on to them for many years, only showing them to a handful of people. Yet, out of the blue, he handed the diagrams over to me and said, "You are the caretaker of these now and they are out of my hands." I was very happy to get the drawings because they were the first real pieces of evidence indicating the channeling phenomenon may be more than pseudo-religious nonsense.

The diagrams themselves are a marvel to behold; they are vividly colored and are done with extreme precision. Many professional people from different fields have examined them, finding them fascinating. Scientists at the University of Chicago have asked me if they could meet the person who drew them, but when I told them the drawings were channeled through a night watchman by an extraterrestrial, and possibly angelic being, I got some pretty strange looks and a "You know what? Forget it" response as they walked away smirking.

It's interesting to note that when these scientists first saw the diagrams, they were amazed and very curious, but as soon I explained how they were done, most wouldn't give them so much as a second glance. The scientists' responses represent a prejudice I've often found in the world of science. According to some contactees, the scientific community's unenthusiastic or dismissive attitude is the reason why ideas and new discoveries are placed in contactees' minds in a very subtle manner, giving us the impression that we ourselves had the ideas. I gave Dr. Hynek the diagrams, and he showed them to a number of well-respected people in the physics and engineering communities. Dr. Hynek reported back to me that all were amazed that a man with such a limited scientific background could produce such diagrams illustrating devices that were beyond the technology of human beings. A professional draftsman told him it would've taken someone with at least twenty years of experience drawing technical diagrams to produce them. He also said that each diagram would take a top-notch professional at least six hours to complete.

Many of the diagrams are devices that were unheard of back in 1968, but are being experimented with today. One device is a three-dimensional viewing screen which back in the late sixties was science fiction, but today is similar to prototypes made for computers. There were also diagrams showing cold fusion, all types of optical test equipment, and communication devices. Also depicted were devices showing propulsion systems using photons (bundles of light energy) and a high-flux resonator for generating energy. One of the most interesting diagrams is an atomic model of the hydrogen nucleus showing it being composed of as many as eight basic particles. If the diagram proves correct, we will have to change our current understanding of atomic physics.

The scientists who looked at the diagrams at Princeton and the University of Chicago are all in agreement that the drawings are accurate in design, but there is not enough information to indicate how they work or how to construct them. One device, called a helical coil, seems to be the simplest of all thirty-two. Using the diagram, an electrical engineer built the coil, and it produced an electromagnetic flux much greater than any similar coils used today. The only problem was that after a short time, the coil burned out and the device stopped functioning. The prototype used an iron core, and when I mentioned this and the coil's limited success to Dean, he seemed to think that the metal core should have been constructed with a beryllium-magnesium alloy.

If the diagrams weren't enough of a mystery, Dean then produced several pages of some unknown language. The symbols were looked at by Dr. John Weston at the University of Tennessee, an expert in linguistics. His opinion was that the symbols are not gibberish, but a complex language composed of over two hundred characters. He believed the language resembled ancient Babylonian, but as far as he could tell, the glyphs are untranslatable into English. Accompanying the text is a short poem in English called "Out Of Orion's Mouth." Below each English word in the text is a series of symbols. The poem served as the Rosetta Stone from which the "alien language" may be interpreted and translated. This translation, in addition to recent information on the symbols, diagrams, and other things Donestra channeled through Dean, appear in chapter ten, "Alien Symbols and Language."

### ENTER APHAX

Dean met another "highly placed being" like Donestra on New Year's Day of 1989. Like Donestra, this being is some type of ascended spirit and is older and more powerful than Donestra—I guess you could say he's Donestra's boss. The being told Dean his name was "Aphax" and he was once a priest who taught philosophy and math in ancient Thebes in 2334 BCE.

Dean's contact with Aphax began with him being taken out of his body and brought to ancient Egypt (possibly Thebes), where he saw a magnificent stone building. He approached the building and saw a small opening. He looked into it and saw a sarcophagus lying prone on a tabletop; he didn't know who was in it. As he watched, the sarcophagus disappeared and was replaced by an image of his father. He continued to watch and his father's image disappeared. Then he saw himself lying there. He broke away from the wall, looking around for Aphax to explain what he was seeing, but was surprised to see that Aphax had turned into a statue and was part of the wall. At that moment, numbers and equations poured into his head, and he was instructed by Aphax to resurrect a lost numerical code that would explain past, present, and future events in the universe.

While sleeping at 3 AM in June of that same year, Dean woke up to see three small, hooded beings enter his room through the doorway. He was not frightened, but he couldn't move. The beings proceeded to do some type of surgical procedure, removing the top part of Dean's skull. He saw several small ruby-colored crystals being put into his brain. The hooded figures completed their task, gathered their equipment (a small surgical kit), and quietly left the same way they entered.

The next morning, Dean began seeing symbols and formulas in his head, and, strangely, he understood what they meant. He wrote them all down on paper. I was able to see the mathematical equations that Dean was working on. Handing them over, he explained that one of them was a mathematical code to predict future events.

To me, everything in the equations looked like chaotic symbols; I didn't understand what he was trying to express. The numbers, letters, and symbols were written down in columns, not in the typical linear fashion of most chemistry and physics equations. Sensing my puzzlement, Dean explained that to solve the problems quickly, they really needed to be projected by laser as a three-dimensional hologram, which, he lamented, he lacked. "The way I keep the columns in order," he said, "is to place symbols in sequence indicating where each line begins, ends, or starts again at the beginning, middle, or end of the equation."

In 2001, I attended a theoretical physics workshop sponsored by MIT and was amazed at the similarity between the equations of chaos theory and Dean Fagerstrom's "celestial equations" I had seen almost twelve years earlier.

For those who might not be familiar with chaos theory, it attempts to explain the fact that "unpredictable" results in a system are actually following a complex pattern, and are therefore predictable. A common example of this is known as the butterfly effect, which states that, in theory, the flutter of a butterfly's wings in China could affect weather patterns in New York City, thousands of miles away. In other words, it's possible that a very small occurrence can predictably produce sometimes drastic results triggered by a series of increasingly significant events.

Chaos theory can also apply to the random selection of numbers in a lottery system. However, in order to successfully predict the wining numbers, one would need to know a constantly changing set of variables each time the lottery's prediction equation is solved. Although these variables can be obtained by observing winning numbers over a period of time, it would be very difficult to plug those numbers into the equation—much too difficult for a humble night watchman . . . but perhaps it would be a simple matter for beings like Donestra or Aphax.

I asked Dean why he didn't just predict the next lottery numbers and make millions; doing so would allow him to concentrate on his "mission" and not worry about his living expenses and the need of a job. Dean replied, "They only let me win as much money as I need. They'll supply numbers for one equation but the numbers won't work a second time. It's impossible to predict the winning numbers unless you have the numbers for the equation."

After he told me about his luck, I went to the store where Dean purchased his lottery tickets, a small gas station and food mart in Putnam Lake. I asked the owner if he knew a Dean Fagerstrom. His answer was, "Yeah, I know him! The guy comes in, plays the lottery, and wins more than anybody I've ever seen—it's weird!"

Over the years, Donestra would teach Dean about "the true nature of the universe." In one of the many lessons he gave Dean, he revealed that our universe is merely a projection of a much larger universe composed entirely of energy. This other universe has been known as the spirit world or "other side" and exists on many different levels. Donestra himself is a sort of angel who was once living in our universe. Donestra was born on June 19, 1647, on Solarian.[4] He left our universe (died) on July 26, 1776, at 129 years old. Donestra is one of three highly placed individuals with a special mission focusing on the development of the human race. I was surprised to learn this—it was the first time I met a contactee who claimed to be in communication not only with an extraterrestrial, but an ET who died and became an angel!

Everything Donestra and Aphax instructed Dean to do has worked out well. None of it has brought Dean any harm; in fact, it has all been beneficial in some way. In the mid-1990s, Donestra appeared before Dean and explained that Franz Liszt, the Austrian composer who was born in 1811 and died in 1886, would play music through him. Dean was instructed to go buy an electric piano, which he did after the beings allowed him to win just enough money in the lottery. He didn't really understand how this was going to happen,

---

4 Solarian doesn't use Earth time measurement; Dean said Donestra always tried to equate things in terms Dean could understand.

since he didn't play the piano. I paid Dean a visit in 1995 and he informed me about his new talent: "I only play to record the music and can only play it once," he said. Dean then played a number of the piano sessions he had taped—they were incredible. I asked Dean if he could play for me live, explaining that someone listening to the tapes might say they were just copied. If I was present when he played, it would be very convincing to even to the most skeptical person.

I pressed Dean about his playing, and while I was still talking, he suddenly sat down at the piano and started playing a beautiful, complicated piece of music. It was amazing to watch this man, who has never had a music lesson in his life, play such an incredible piece. When he finished I asked him, "What just happened?" Dean explained that he had no idea, but can usually feel it coming on, which is why he has the recorder all set up and ready to go. To date, Dean has recorded two hundred different compositions, all of which he claims were channeled by Liszt.

Dean gave me two of the tapes he produced, and through a friend, the tapes were played for a music expert at the Julliard School of Music in New York City.[5] The person was a good friend of a professor at the school; I asked if he would listen to a taped piano performance because I wanted to know the style of the player and the piece. After five seconds of listening, the professor exclaimed, "Stop! It's Franz Liszt!" The rest of the tape was played for him and his conclusions

---

5 The Juilliard School, located at the Lincoln Center for the Performing Arts in New York City, is a very elite performing arts conservatory.

were that it was definitely Liszt, but a piece he had never heard before. He concluded by saying, "Whoever is playing is a master piano player, a virtuoso. Usually, you need at least twenty years of practice to emulate Liszt's style." As interesting contrast, I also played the tape for the (now-deceased) UFO researcher and author of *Silent Invasion*, Ellen Crystall. Ellen had a doctorate in music and wasn't very impressed when she heard the recording. She said, "Anyone with piano experience could just punch out the piece on the tape." However, the key phrase here is "piano experience"—remember that Dean had none.

As lucky and fortunate as Dean may have seemed, from the luck in the lottery to his incredible music ability, I'll never forget one of the last things he said to me about his contact with these angelic beings: he wasn't in control of the communication. Donestra and/or Aphax would do whatever they wanted, whenever they wanted, and Dean admitted that at times, he felt a little burned out.

In the years that followed, Dean produced a number of smaller diagrams I believe may be the missing parts of the main diagrams he drew almost forty years before. Although each plate is incredible-looking, once again there isn't enough information to fully understand what the technology is used for or how it works.

I stayed in touch with Dean until 2007, when he fell ill and had to be hospitalized. He's now in a specialized facility that provides the care he needs. Dean's legacy is still with us, and if I had to pick one case that convinced me about the possibility of extraterrestrial contacts, it would be the incredible experiences of Mr. J. Dean Fagerstrom.

## Monka Meets Donestra

In my gathering information on the contact experience from people who claim to channel extraterrestrials and other beings, I've noticed that the same or similar entity names keep popping up. One being named "Monka" has manifested more than a few times in the past thirty years. The first time I heard Monka's name was in the early eighties, when the channeling phenomenon was new to me. It's important I mention this case—it serves as evidence that the people involved may have been in actual contact with a nonhuman intelligence from another plane of existence.

Shortly after my first meeting with Dean Fagerstrom in 1982, I received a letter from a couple who at the time lived in Greenwich, Connecticut. The letter explained that they had been channeling a number of extraterrestrial entities for several years and would like to know if I was willing to be present during of their sessions. The letter went on to say that they were in contact with not one, but a hundred and four different types of extraterrestrials, who belong to a sort of federation of planets. The couple's first names are Mark and Lois, last names withheld.

Mark and Lois had been channeling "extraterrestrials" at their home for several years using a method called automatic writing.[6] I gave them a call and made an appointment to meet with them at their home in December of that year.

---

6 Automatic writing is the process in which a person produces information in the written form that does not come from the writer's conscious thoughts. According to those who have done automatic writing, they are unaware of what will be written. In some cases,

I arrived in the early evening and was greeted by the couple and their dog, a mixed Shetland collie that seemed very friendly and gentle. We all went into the living room and got to know each other a little better before the contact attempt was made. As we were introducing ourselves, we were joined by a young woman Mark introduced as a gifted psychic. This young woman was interested in the communications and often sat in on sessions. I was prepared to ask everyone my standard questions, ones that have helped me weed out charlatans from honest people in the past, but nothing could have prepared me for what would take place over the next several hours.

The method of communication was simple: Lois would hold a pencil and some paper on her lap, and Mark would touch her hand lightly. Lois would then feel what to write on the paper; her hand at times would move by itself, apparently under the entity's control. While physical contact isn't traditionally necessary for channeling, communication couldn't be established for Mark and Lois unless Mark gently rested his hand on top of Lois's writing hand. They said that the combination of their energies provided the power the extraterrestrials needed to communicate. I asked if this was the only method of communication, and Mark replied,

---

the writing is done by people in a trance state. In others, the writer is aware of their surroundings but is not in control of their writing hand. Messages that allegedly came from the spirit world were popular in the nineteenth century, but in modern times, even more people are claiming to receive messages from aliens and higher beings from other dimensions.

"Yes, but they promised in the near future to channel voice information through one of us."

Everyone sat in a circle as the couple attempted the communication. After a moment, Lois's arm began to twitch. Mark, feeling the tension, stated that contact had been made with one or more extraterrestrials. As soon as contact was established, the dog that was once friendly and gentle became very nervous and almost vicious. She had a strange glare in her eyes as she watched me, and every time I moved, she looked at me and growled. Before the communication, the dog's eyes were gentle and soft, but now they were glaring and were a very angry, deep black that seemed to glow in the dim light. I also noticed that the hair on the dog's back was standing up, and she whined and cried as if frightened of something. There was no doubt in my mind that the communication was somehow affecting the animal in a very negative way. I asked if the dog ever reacted like this before and the answer from all present was no, this was the first time it had ever happened.

As the communication continued, Mark asked, "Who is in touch with us tonight?" A number of beings then "signed in." According to Mark and Lois, some of them were frequent visitor, Mark and Lois were very familiar with, while some of the others very rarely communicated. Listed below are the beings' names and a brief description of who they are, and in some cases, where they are from.

> **Monka:** A sort of priest/philosopher who resides underground in the pyramids of Mars. He is also called the "Protector of Earth." Monka is not a physical being,

but a being of energy that lives in another dimension on the red planet.

**Fanta One:** Not much was said about this one, though I did find out Fanta One was not one individual being, but at least fifty that work together and belong to a federation of planets.

**Nemus:** A scientist from this federation of planets.

**Soltec:** A sort of mystic priest.

**Wan:** Resides in the core of the Earth. Home planet is called Lumina in the Andromeda galaxy. He is a nuclear physicist.

**Han:** Wan's mate who lives with Han in the Earth's core with their five-year-old son, Eot. Han is an endocrinologist.

**Lomu:** An artist from the Lomu system close to the star Sirius in the constellation of Canis Major. Lomu channels sketches through Lois in the event a visual representation is needed.

**Zar:** A healer or doctor from the Lumina system.

**Kalira:** A politician or leader from the Lumina system.

**Urso:** A military leader and captain of a giant ship that often visits Earth. Origin unknown.

The channeling session began with Monka greeting us, "In the light of the radiant one." Most of the communications that came through were of little value to me as a scientist. The beings tactfully steered away from hard scientific questions and were more concerned with teaching philosophy and New Age ideas. If a question was asked about science, either Han or Nemus would answer. If a question was poised about religion, Monka or Soltec would answer. If a diagram was needed, Lomu would take over. The actual content of the communication is not important in this case; what's important are the physical manifestations that began taking place.

Five minutes after the communications began, the temperature of the room began to drop. Before the session, the temperature was seventy-six, and now, when the communications began, it dropped down to fifty-six. Although the heat was blasting out of the vent and the thermostat was turned up to eighty-five degrees, the room temperature remained cold and as the night went on, continued to drop. After a while, the air became so cold we could see our breath! The young woman introduced as a psychic complained of a great deal of pain in her head and drifted into a semi-conscious state. Eventually she became so ill that a friend had to come and take her home. The dog was also reacting to what was going on: what was once a calm and friendly animal was now terrified and sat in front of me the entire time with its eyes fixed on me as if ready to attack.

I definitely felt as if there was some force in the room draining energy not only from people, but also from the molecules in the air. I was the only one who really didn't seem affected by it. As the communications continued, a warning came through Monka that a very negative being and very powerful evil force was trying to destroy me because I was coming too close to discovering his true identity.

During the session the phone rang, but no one was on the line; we heard a strange knocking on the window, and a number of unusual sounds that resembled a very low chanting coming from outside or from another room. When I asked the being Soltec if he could manifest something in the room, a teapot on the kitchen stove flew off crashing to the floor, making a very loud noise. As strange as this may already seem, the communications with Monka and his group took an even more bizarre turn.

As Lois was writing information from Monka, her hand began to shake and it seemed as if she was losing control of it. This shaking was new to them and they seemed surprised and almost fearful. Then, without warning, a message came in from another source. A brief transcript is provided below:

**Mark:** Who is this, please?
**Unknown Being:** I will speak only to Phil.
**Phil:** Well, can you tell me who you are?
**Unknown Being:** Donestra.

*(I was quite amazed—this was without a doubt the same Donestra that Dean Fagerstrom claimed to be in contact with. There is no way Mark and Lois could have known about his contact with Mr. Fagerstrom and the diagrams he had instructed Dean to turn over to me.)*

**Phil:** Donestra, what the hell am I supposed to do with these diagrams?!
**Donestra:** In time, you will know. You must, however, be warned that a very ancient evil force has been trying to get to you for a very long time. You are old enemies with this being, and have defeated him many times in the past. I cannot hold this line of communication.

Donestra faded out, and Monka and the others returned.

**Nemus, Fanta One, Wan, and Lomu:** Who was that? I think he had trouble getting through.

**Monka:** He is a very high order of being. He used me as a medium to channel his information through Lois so that Phil could get it. I have never encountered this before. I must find out more information and must end this communication session now.

At that point, the session ended and everyone felt exhausted except me. It seems Donestra used Monka to channel information to the group, something I don't think anyone, including myself, was expecting. When the channeling session ended, the temperature of the room returned to normal. As I got out of the chair and prepared to leave, the dog was once again friendly and calm.

Believe it or not, the story doesn't end here. In the months to follow, I would visit Mark and Lois several times, but after that night, the communication was never quite the same and Monka refused to channel any information in my presence.

Shortly after my encounter with Monka and his gang, a new channeling group invited me to a session. They consisted of a number of people who gather at a Connecticut home to contact a number of extraterrestrials that call themselves "the Ring." The Ring is another federation of planets that try to impart wisdom and information to us, the poor "underdeveloped beings of planet Earth." Although the Ring sessions seem harmless to potential attendees, they claim you will receive the knowledge of these space brothers only as long as you pay your two-hundred-dollar fee. I found no evidence that groups like the Ring are in contact with an extraterrestrial intelligence.

In one channeling session with another popular group called "the Gathering," the extraterrestrials promised to channel a number of diagrams that would serve as blueprints for a device that would allow direct communication with them. After several sessions, no diagrams had been channeled, and I became a little impatient. At what was to be my final session, I asked about the diagrams. The answer was, "We will be sending them within the next six months, but you must be present at every session to learn more about the true nature of the universe." Hearing this, I became frustrated and asked why I had to wait such a long time. I asked, "Why does the information have to be channeled? There's no guarantee I'll be able to build this device anyway. Why don't you (the aliens) just come down here in one of your spaceships, drop it off somewhere, and I'll pick it up? Think of all the time we'll save." Well, that was the wrong comment to make! Soon after, the communication abruptly ceased, and I was shown the door. Unsurprisingly, I was never asked back to another Gathering channeling session.

# FOUR

# ENCOUNTERS OF
# THE FOURTH KIND

Encounters of the fourth kind are increasing worldwide. When looking at the reports made to the many UFO research organizations including the Intruders Foundation, the UFO Reporting Center, the Center for UFO Studies, and the Mutual UFO Network, it seems obvious. The problem is that some of these alien abduction claims aren't investigated by the larger organizations because many reports sound too incredible to believe. At least one of the organizations mentioned above released a statement that they would not investigate wild or bizarre claims, in the interest of keeping the study of UFOs respectable and scientific. When I read about their new policy, I thought, "Come on, guys! Really, there's little science in what we do already. You're looking for spaceships and aliens on Earth *and* you want respect from the scientific community? It's not going to happen in this day and age!" It is my firm belief that all contact claims—no matter how strange or outlandish—should be investigated. We must remember that in most cases, a witness's interpretation of the event may make the experience sound too incredible to believe. It is the task of the investigator to weed out facts from the experiencer's fiction and fears.

## They're Here!

This case study takes us back to 1992 and involves a young couple I'll refer to as Maria and George, who lived in Newburgh, New York. Maria and George both had previous histories with the paranormal before they met each other, but after they married, things escalated.

As a child, Maria remembers seeing ghosts around her father. The ghosts sometimes would visit her at night and take her away, returning her to her room after several hours had passed. As a teen, after one visit from the "ghosts," Maria suddenly developed an irritating eye twitch. Her mother took her to the doctor, who discovered a piece of silicone embedded in her lower eyelid. The doctor was very puzzled as to how it could have gotten there, and as far as I know, there was no type of analysis done on the chip—the doctor just threw it away.

As for George, he had recurring dreams of strange places and structures at a very early age that were so vivid, he would wake up in the morning and promptly draw what he had seen. George has always had a fascination with pyramids because he often saw them in his dreams. He remembers the dream pyramids being so real and detailed that he felt compelled to try to build one. It was as if a telepathic message was placed in his mind and he was compelled to construct what he saw. Shortly after his dream, George had a friend approach him who also had a fascination with pyramids. Although George didn't tell this person about his dreams, the friend insisted that he work with him to construct a large pyramid made out of glass and metal. Although the pyramid was never constructed, he still wanted to build one, so he started constructing a number of miniature models.

While growing up, George had two UFO sightings in which he saw strange lights in the sky perform amazing flights of acrobatics. He felt the sightings were staged for him and that some type of telepathic connection was formed between him and the UFOs. After he met Maria, he tried to forget about the UFOs and the other strange occurrences he had experienced all his life. However, it wasn't until they married that both their lives would take a very bizarre turn.

George feels he has been chosen by an alien intelligence to perform some function in the future. He was told in a dream that these aliens will come for him and take him away "when the stars fall out of the sky." Since their marriage, the couple claims that a number of small gray beings with very large eyes have come into their home and abducted them on numerous occasions. After the visits, Maria and George would wake up in the morning feeling very tired, but they've never found any marks on their bodies. The visitation take place with such great frequency that George feels he can predict when they are going to have a visit from the alien creatures—his body will start to "tingle." Maria, too, has grown used to seeing beings and will say to George, "Your friends are here." She calls them "friends" because George actually feels the beings mean no harm and have come to help them.

George and Maria have a daughter who is almost two years old. One day, she brought out her doll and asked her mother to open its head. Maria asked her where she got an idea like that, and she told her, "They do it to Daddy at night." The child has also pointed to pictures of alien beings on book and magazine covers and has indicated knowing that they've entered their house.

Like most people who experience some type of paranormal phenomena, there are several electromagnetic disturbances in their home. Clocks don't work properly, light bulbs explode, and appliances malfunction for no apparent reason. Stranger still, the phone rings several times during the day and night with no one on the line, though sometimes a strange beeping sound is heard. Although they have caller ID, the mysterious caller's number never displays.

George recounts a time when he was still living with his parents, and a friend was staying with him. As this friend left the house that evening, he saw blue globes of light enter the window to George's room. The friend also says that on more than one occasion, he has seen these blue lights "enter" George's sleeping body. After Maria and George married, the lights didn't go away—they both saw them at least once a week, flying around their apartment, passing right through the windows and walls.

George and Maria have been abducted a number of times, the scenario of which is always the same: the beings enter their bedroom and approach them. The next thing George and Maria know, it's morning. After reviewing the case and the hours of audio tape, I have come to the conclusion that the alien intelligence seems to be more interested in Maria than George. Maria generally has more of a recollection of seeing the beings than George, and while George seems to welcome the visitations, Maria is fearful of the beings. The intelligence could be using George to keep Maria calm so the abductions can happen smoothly, but the big question is, why are they interested in Maria? I could speculate on this, but will leave the final conclusion up to the reader.

My last session with George and Maria was in the late 1990s; a well-known UFO investigator was with me at the time. In the interview, I asked Maria specific details about her abduction experiences, and what she said next shocked us both. When I asked Maria if she saw any other human beings onboard the craft when she was there, she kept staring at the person who was with me. Eventually, she said, "I wasn't going to mention it, but I saw you on the ship a number of times, strapped to a table." My coinvestigator's face paled and she shakily replied, "I always had dreams of what you're describing to Phil, but I thought they were nothing more than that. Yes, I had dreams of being onboard an alien craft as a child and adult. The dreams made me interested in finding out more." Needless to say, this was an unexpected turn in the investigation! Unfortunately, my coinvestigator, who had become quite well known as a paranormal researcher in the eighties and nineties, suddenly stopped pursuing her interest in UFOs sometime later. I've since lost all contact with her.

### Encounter on the Hill

The next case took place in 1984 during the peak of UFO and paranormal activity in the Hudson Valley. This episode involved a close encounter, missing time, and abduction. If real, the implications of the following experience are fantastic. There is no doubt in my mind that the witness involved is telling the truth.

"Bill" was at the time a thirty-two-year-old computer programmer for a major scientific engineering corporation that helped design and build components for the NASA Hubble Space Telescope. On July 19, 1984, at about 10:30 PM, Bill left his job in Norwalk, Connecticut. By eleven, he was heading west on I-84, just west of the New York–Connecticut border. As he approached the turn-off to the Taconic Parkway in Dutchess County, he noticed a very bright, almost circular object in the northern sky. The lights seemed to be hovering there, not moving at all, and were a very bright white. Bill counted seven in total.

Bill slowed his car and tried to study the lights closely, which proved difficult because he was still driving and the lights were off to his right. After a moment, the lights appeared to move to the left, and it was at this time he noticed a dark mass behind them, silhouetted against the brighter light-polluted sky. He continued to drive west on I-84 and soon lost sight of the object. He tried to push the sighting out of his mind. "Oh," he said to himself. "It must have been those guys from Stormville Airport flying those ultralight planes in formation, trying to fake a UFO." Bill arrived at that conclusion because previous sightings in that area had been explained away by federal and state authorities as being nothing more than a group of pilots flying stunt planes (an explanation, of course, that was never proven to be the cause of the sightings that took place between 1983 and 1989). Bill continued driving home and listening to the radio as he went along, starting to forget about what he had just seen moments before.

Bill turned off at the Route 52 exit and traveled north. The time was now close to 11:15 PM and the roads were quite deserted. He came to a clearing and noticed a large, dark mass sitting about two hundred yards from the road. At first he thought it was a new home, but then realized there couldn't be a house there because he had gone that way just the night before and the field had been empty. In fact, he realized, he always drove home that way and there never had been any type of structure in that field before. Bill slowed his car to get a better look. "This object was huge and dark," he said. "It was almost the same shape as a long barn . . . the kind used for raising chickens, but it seemed more tapered towards the sides. It was very smooth." As he watched, the dark object rose noiselessly into the air. Bill felt pretty upset because his was the only car on the road. The object rose higher and higher, and Bill could now see that it looked a black triangle hovering about a hundred feet above the ground. It was now about twice as high as the trees and moving slowly toward Bill, who was still in the car, moving at a crawl. He says his radio started to "sound funny," like music from a tape player with very weak batteries; the voices and the music all sounded distorted and out of tune.

Frightened, Bill stepped on the gas pedal and sped away from the still-approaching object. His heart was racing almost as fast as his car as he drove up the road at more than seventy miles per hour. He lost sight of the object and slowed down a bit—he was in a 35 mph zone. After driving for several minutes, he noticed a bright white glow over the hill ahead. As he approached the crest of the hill, he was shocked to see the object waiting there for him! It was about three hundred feet above the trees and was completely lit up with rows of white and yellow lights. Bill was sure this was the same object he had seen earlier in the field, but this time, the lights outlined a very large craft that without a doubt was triangular in shape. Bill knew this object was after him. How he knew this he's not sure, but he felt it strongly.

Bill stopped his car and turned off the engine and lights. He was hoping that whoever was in the thing would not see him, and go away. He felt very strongly that the UFO had tracked him and isolated him on the road and was now going to "capture" him. The UFO turned off all its lights and Bill could still see its large triangular shape hovering in the sky. The UFO then started moving slowly towards him without a sound, and as it passed directly over the car, he saw that it had quite a detailed underside, with a great network of grids and strange circular areas that looked like portals. Bill told me, "I really don't want to make the comparison, but the UFO looked like one of those star destroyers from the movie *Star Wars*. The underside was triangular, but I didn't see the top of the craft, so I can't tell you what shape it was." While examining the UFO's underside,

Bill noticed areas that looked like tunnels leading into the object. Inside these circular areas, lights were flashing in a strobe-like manner. Bill estimated the object to be at least three hundred feet long and more than two hundred feet above his car.

The last thing Bill recalls was watching the UFO pass over the car. Then it was gone. The strange thing was he did not see it fully clear his car, it just vanished! Stranger still, Bill's car was not in the same place as when he first saw the UFO. Bill and his car were now six hundred feet down the hill he had driven up when he first saw the object. He was positive that it was 11:30 PM when he first saw the UFO, but when he looked at his clock again, it was now almost one in the morning. The entire sighting from when he first saw the glow beyond the hill to when the object passed over his car seemed like no more than ten to fifteen minutes, yet at least one hour had passed. Bill got into his car and drove home feeling very tired and uneasy; he also had a very stiff neck and a headache. He told me his neck was so stiff, it was almost impossible for him to drive.

When Bill arrived home, he told his wife about the sighting. She was worried to begin with because he was more than an hour late. Later that night, Bill woke up suddenly screaming, "Get away from me! Get away from me!" His wife told me that since the night of the sighting, he's been afraid to go out after dark. He even insisted that his boss keep him off the evening or night shift at his job. After the initial shock had worn off, Bill wanted to find out more about the UFO experience and his resulting nightmares.

It wasn't until 1987 that Bill contacted me and told his story. He had seen Budd Hopkins talk about alien abductions and missing time on a TV talk show. Bill asked me if it would be possible to have himself hypnotized so he could find out what happened in that hour of lost time. Hearing Hopkins speak about the subject of abduction made Bill fearful and he wanted to make sure that he wasn't an abductee himself.

I arranged to have Bill meet with an area psychologist in the area to whom I've referred many people for regressive hypnosis. After completing a psychological profile, the doctor determined that Bill was sane, but had considerable psychological trauma due to his paranormal experience (the UFO sighting). The following is a transcript of Bill's encounter while under hypnosis. He first talks about seeing the lights while driving on I-84 and then the dark object in the field, after which his voice becomes filled with emotion and fear. I have edited out the therapist's questions and prompts in the transcript.

**Bill:** I see it now . . . it's that thing! It's coming over in my direction! I'm going to turn the lights off on the car so maybe they won't see me and they will go away. It's huge . . . oh my God, what is it? There is someone standing in the road and he's walking toward the car. "Who are you," I scream. He says to me, "Do not be fearful. We need you, you have been selected." "Selected for what?" . . . Get away! I feel strange, like I am floating in air. It's all dark. I am now on this table and these guys are all around me. There are six of them. Two are at my head and two on the sides. My legs and arms are like dead weights, I can't move them.

*Bill is then asked to describe the beings in greater detail.*

**Bill:** These guys are small. They have large heads with round, black eyes, the eyes are so black . . . I can't see any pupils. They look like shark eyes, they don't even look real. They are dressed in some type of black and white skintight suit that look like diving suits. I can't see their hands and the one near my head is moving some type of thing up and down the side of my head—it looks like a portable vacuum cleaner. He's moving it closer and it's making my head vibrate. It feels like a drill going through my head . . . STOP IT! STOP! IT HURTS! What are you doing to me? Will somebody please help me? This can't be real. They are looking for something and they found it, I can't hear them speak, but I know what they are saying. I can feel my legs and arms now and they are allowing me to get up. They only come up to the lower part of my chest and they are very skinny (Bill is 6' 1"). They look like human bugs with big black eyes and now I can see their hands . . . they look more like claws with three fingers on each hand.

The others are now over some type of panel. Two of them are leading me by my arms. They ask me not to look around and to keep my eyes straight ahead . . . something about radiation from the sides of the ship hurting my eyes. Where are you from? . . . I don't understand. One of them said in my mind, "We are from here." I am asking them if they are going to let me go . . . he says, "Yes, but we shall see you again." He is telling me they come from a place which is very ugly in comparison to Earth and they would like to live here but they can't. I'm telling him that I will remember everything and tell people what is going on but he just can't take a person like this and experiment with them because it's against the law. He's telling me that they *do* have the right to do it, and no one is getting hurt. He is now telling me that I will remember some of what has taken place but there are forces that will stop me from telling others what happened."

Bill then found himself back in his car and now remembered every aspect of the experience, which to him was very real. To this day, he is fearful that the strange creatures who abducted him on his way home will come back for him. In my investigation into Bill's case, I was puzzled as to why there was no traffic on Route 52 during his experience. Although the area's population isn't as dense as other nearby towns, there should have been many more cars on the road; I-84 is a major road in the county. Later, I discovered that during the time of Bill's abduction, the road was closed off on one end. One motorist who traveled the road nightly said that when he drove off the exit ramp for Route 52, there was a road block with two or three men in coveralls waving cars to a side-road detour. He couldn't get a close look at the men, but said they were in yellow outfits with hard hats, holding glowing rods rather than flash lights. I then called the Dutchess and Putnam county road working crews and was told that no county workers were at that location and that they don't work at night, except during emergencies. I also contacted the state highway crew, the local electric companies, and the gas and telephone companies but still couldn't find out who was responsible for the road block. State police and local law enforcement were also of no help.

Perhaps the road was blocked off by the intelligence in the UFO, the same intelligence that abducted Bill. The purpose might have been to isolate him so he could be abducted with no witnesses present. In reviewing the case, what bothered me is that the people who blocked the road off were reported to be quite human-looking. Over the years I would continue to receive reports in which human beings (or human-looking beings) were used by alien intelligence to assist in the abduction of people.

## Transported Through the Rockies

The next abduction case was given to me in the early eighties. It involved a truck driver named David who, with his girlfriend, Lia, had an encounter with an alien craft and contact with alien beings while driving in Colorado.

On November 29, 1981, David and Lia were heading back to New York from a vacation in California. It was a clear, chilly night, and the moon was full as they drove through Colorado, thirty miles from the entrance to the Rockies. There was going to be a total lunar eclipse that night, so both wanted to be up in the mountains to see it better.

They were driving on a flat, straight road when David looked up and saw a bright red star slowly move across the sky. He thought at first it was a satellite, but then it stopped and shot straight down below the horizon. He thought that was strange, and wondered what it was because no satellite or aircraft could possibly do what he saw the red light do. After about five minutes, both noticed another ball of light, but this one shot up from the horizon and then moved slowly overhead. As it reached the point directly above the couple, it began to move at the same speed as the car, making it appear motionless.

David described the object as resembling a red ball of light and added that it was impossible to tell how high the UFO was, but he guessed it was two thousand feet or so above the ground. No matter how much he tried speeding up or slowing down, the object stayed directly over the car. Lia added that it looked like it was spying on them and that she felt some kind of telepathic communication with the object; she suddenly yelled out "they want to capture us," while David tried to make an escape. Both say they became frightened—there was no one else on the road. The UFO followed them for another ten miles and then suddenly streaked backward. They lost sight of it. David, still shaken, continued driving and turned on the radio, hoping the music would take their minds off of what just happened.

After listening to the music for half an hour, the radio reception became staticky and distorted. David's first thought was that perhaps the mountains were blocking the signal. He looked in the rearview mirror and saw a distant light on the road approach very quickly. It was getting brighter and brighter and then all of a sudden—*flash!*— it was right behind them, about ten feet off the ground. David described the object as being some type of disc that glowed white in the center and red around its edges. The object was about three times the size of their car and moved completely silently. David described the lights as being a sort of fluorescent white and red, and they couldn't see any windows.

David floored the gas pedal and was now going ninety miles per hour, yet the strange object kept the same distance from the car with seemingly no effort at all. The object maintained its distance, about ten feet behind car, regardless of whether David slowed down or sped up again. Lia panicked and screamed that the object was a UFO, and that the aliens onboard wanted to take them. David thought that perhaps the two of them were going to be kidnapped and put in a zoo on another planet. As he watched the UFO in the rearview mirror, a figure appeared at the very front of the ship. David says, "It was strange . . . it was as if this being was always there but was hidden behind the light. When it came very close to the front, I could see the figure's outline very clearly."

He described the "alien" as being very slim with a large head and large, slanted eyes that seemed to glow yellow despite the creature hiding behind the ship's lights. David then heard a voice in his head say, "You will not be harmed. We are interested in studying you and the female." He said that when he heard the voice there was also a loud buzzing sound inside his head. David yelled out, "I don't care who or what you are! If you want to communicate with the human race, then why pick us?! Get away, we don't know anything!" The car was now traveling very fast, and they were approaching the entrance to the Rockies. The eclipse was just beginning when suddenly, David and Lia found themselves on the east side of the Rockies. The eclipse was over and the moon was setting in the west. David was shocked to see a sign in front of them: "Denver." The couple, along with the car, seemed to have been transported *through* the Rocky Mountains! They continued to drive, hardly speaking to each other, and stopped at the nearest motel. They both took showers, feeling unclean and extremely tired. They stayed at the motel overnight and left for New York in the morning. The rest of the trip was uneventful.

It seems David and Lia experienced at least four hours of missing time. I believe this is an unusual abduction because the car was also taken. The mileage on the car only showed an eighteen-mile difference between the time of the close encounter with the UFO and when the couple found themselves on the east side of the Rocky Mountains, but in actuality, this is a distance of over a hundred and fifty miles! I also questioned the couple about the amount of gas in their car, and it seems they still had almost three quarters of a tank.

Neither person had marks on their bodies, but both suffered from insomnia in the six months after the encounter. David told me that every time he closed his eyes, he would see flashes of some alien creature that looked like a giant insect with a large, long head and slanted yellow eyes looking down on him. David continued to have paranormal experiences, and on more than one occasion claimed that "the aliens" came into his room at night to take him aboard their ship. When taken to the ship, they would place him on a black table and scan his body up and down with a device that looked like a handheld vacuum cleaner with a short nozzle on it. In 1999, David moved to Montana with the hope that the creatures would not find him. I lost contact with him after he moved and have no idea if his encounters continued. His girlfriend moved to California shortly after the abduction experience in the Rockies and it's unknown if she continued to have encounters with the yellow-eyed beings.

# FIVE

# NIGHT VISITORS

My research has shown that the strangest, most bizarre occurrences take place at around three in the morning. I think the majority of paranormal investigators will agree with this and wonder along with me what the attraction of three o'clock in the morning is. The number of cases involving alien-like beings and shadow people entering the bedrooms of people in the wee hours of the morning seems to be on the rise. The story presented below comes from an individual who, for most of his life, has experienced paranormal events, up to and including repeated abductions. I investigated this case between 1987 and 1992; it remains unexplained.

## The Image

The experiencer is an elderly gentleman named Bob, a successful corporate executive who at the time lived alone in a remodeled farmhouse in Bethel, Connecticut. For a number of months he had been awakened in the early morning hours by a presence he'd previously encountered many times in his

life. The events would occur several times a month, beginning with a face appearing in the manner of a holographic
image on the wall. The face was usually red and pear-shaped,
with long, slanted eyes, no chin or ears, and a very small
mouth. As soon as the face materialized, Bob would always
black out and wake up the next day, sometimes with a headache, other times feeling fine.

Bob has a heart condition and during one of these encounters, just after seeing the face, he fell into a light trance
and felt hands all over his body. The hands seemed to move
him around and he couldn't open his eyes. He tried speaking to whoever was attached to the hands, asking them if
they could please fix his heart while they were messing with
his body. Once he made his request, Bob felt a warm sensation all over his body, relaxing him and sending him off to a
deep sleep. He woke up the next day with no ill effects and
felt quite good.

Bob had an appointment with his doctor the day after he
asked the "aliens" to fix his heart, and he decided to mention the strange things that had been happening to him at
night. His doctor then told him to come back in a couple
of days for another examination without responding to the
rest of his story at all. Later, Bob received a phone call saying that his next appointment would be at Yale University's
medical school where a number of experts would review his
case.

Bob drove to Yale–New Haven Medical Center for his appointment, whereupon his doctor took him into a room of a
handful of people (all doctors, he assumed) sitting in chairs

arranged in a semicircle. Bob took a seat and the doctors began asking him questions about his nighttime encounters with the beings. After about an hour, his doctor escorted him out. He asked her why he had been questioned like that, and she told him they were interested in him as experts in various scientific and medical fields. She explained that she wanted a number of different opinions and that she had to make sure the medication he was taking was not having any strange, adverse effects on him. Bob went home more puzzled about the events than before—he felt that some of the people at the meeting didn't act or look like doctors; they seemed more like government agents.

In addition to the strange alien "face" appearing on his bedroom wall, Bob also had a number of other paranormal events take place in his home, including the appearance of ghost-like shadow figures in the house, witnessed by a number of people; poltergeist activity in the form of independently moving chairs and objects; unidentifiable, strange sounds; and burned, brown marks that appeared on his lawn in the weeks and months following the "face's" first appearance. A brief investigation into Bob's past indicates that as a young man, Bob experienced and witnessed a number of paranormal occurrences, including UFO sightings. I also discovered Bob's daughter may have also had similar experiences, but she wasn't willing to talk about them.

I visited Bob several times at his home and saw the aforementioned brown spots on his lawn, and on one occasion, I also heard a strange humming noise while in the house. I tried tracking down the source of the noise for at least an hour, but never found it. The sound seemed to come from every section of the house and I could find no electrical or mechanical source for it. It was like an electric current resonating through fine quartz crystal, and the unusual thing was that although it was very audible, the sound wouldn't record on my cassette recorder. I believe the strange sound was some type of energy surge—could it be related to one that caused a dimensional portal to open, thereby allowing strange beings to enter our universe?

The next step in my investigation was to set up an electromagnetic detector wired through a chart recorder and an oscilloscope to record and analyze the frequency and the origin of the noise, but before I could set up the instruments, the sound stopped and was never heard again. As far as I know, after the sound stopped, Bob never saw the faces again. To this day, the being with the red face has left him alone.

## The Travelers

Since the 1960s, the contact phenomenon has become more widespread and includes people from all walks of life and levels of education. In the mid-1990s, I received a call from a man who at the time was a geologist who claimed he was "escorted by aliens" into some kind of dimensional ship where he saw not only other aliens, but hybrid human-aliens. I arranged to meet the man soon after his call; he seemed very eager to tell me his story.

"It was late April in 1996 and I decided to go to bed early. For some reason, I was feeling very tired but it wasn't tiredness from the day—it was like I had just taken a sleeping pill. I went to bed and in a matter of minutes, fell into a deep sleep. I woke up with a jump and heard a buzzing in the room. I looked at the clock—it was 2:45 AM. I tried to figure out where the buzzing sound was coming from when without warning, the wall on the north side of the bedroom started to glow with a faint, dull, yellow color. I sat up in bed, wondering what the hell was going on. Then, this being walked right through the wall, like it was liquid or something. I was really shocked, because 'he' looked like one of the gray-type aliens they show in UFO movies, books, and magazines.

"He was about five feet tall or so and his skin was paper-white, not gray. He had a large head and round, black eyes. He appeared to be in a black, skin-tight suit, and his arms were longer than you would expect for someone of that size. I couldn't see his fingers. The alien had no visible ears and I could barely see his mouth; his lips were very thin. He walked over to the bed and began speaking to me. I didn't actually hear him speak out loud; I heard his voice inside my head. He said, 'Don't be afraid, I come in peace. I want to show you something you will have to learn. In the future, you will be in a position to help us.' Now, this was a little strange because I actually didn't have any fear at all. The strange-looking visitor radiated peace and good will; I felt very easy with him . . . at least I think it was a 'him.' I got out of bed, followed the alien and we went right through the wall. I then found myself in a small, very dark room that looked like an elevator. The being told me we were in a type of vehicle that was able to travel through space and time.

We were in this room for . . . well, I really don't know how long, because I had no sense of time. There was no sense of motion or anything like that, no noise, nothing. It must have been a short time because I can't remember any conversations with the being at that point. I did ask him what his name was, and he replied, 'Names are not used. We identify each other by telepathic signatures in our thoughts.'

"Suddenly we were in a lit corridor. I looked up for lights, but didn't see any. Somehow, the entire room was lit in a whitish light that reminded me of the fluorescent lights in hospitals. We stopped, there was a flash of light, and suddenly we were in a very large room with tables. I looked towards the far end and saw a man and a woman on separate tables, lying head-to-head. I knew who they were, but as I think about it now, I can't remember where from. But while I was there seeing them lying on the tables, I knew even their names. The woman had long, black hair and she turned her head to greet me. She smiled and greeted the being, 'Hi, we're fine.' I asked the being why they were here and he said, 'This man and woman volunteered to help us. We have many people who are helping us.' I then asked the being where he was from and he told me he was from another star system; his species has the ability to travel in the closer dimensional windows to our planet.

"I saw a number of unusually tall men wearing lab coats, and from the back, they appeared human. The being then told me he had to leave and one of the human-like beings came over and greeted me. This other being had black hair and very round, dark eyes. He looked almost human to me, but something was a little off. He spoke in English and told me he was a hybrid between the human race and the beings he called 'the Travelers.' I asked him if he had a name and he said, 'No. We have signatures in our brains.' He told me he was a scientist who was trained and educated in Earth's medical schools and by the Travelers. He revealed that there are many like him on our planet—some closer to being human and some more like the Travelers. He then said, 'Those who more closely resemble humans are returned to your planet to live in your world. At a certain age, we contact them to help us with the mission. Those who are genetically closer to the travelers like me stay on these ships to work. We are all involved in an important mission, and that is to save a race of ancient beings.'

"The other 'doctors' in the room didn't pay attention to me and seemed quite involved in their work. Although I couldn't see exactly what they were working on, I did see something on one of the tables move, so whatever they were working on was alive. The hybrid man speaking to me had a strange, monotonous, unemotional voice and his face was always straight and devoid of emotion. I got the feeling he was dead serious about what he was explaining.

"I asked him to show me what the doctors in the lab coats were working on, and he took me over to a table that looked like it was made of sterile stainless steel. The table had a number of instruments that looked like medical monitors with digital readouts. As I walked over to the table, I was shocked to see a hybrid baby on the table with a number of tubes attached to him. I say 'him' because it was clearly a male. The child must have been no more than a month old, but it wasn't quite human. I mean, it had human features but also looked like the being that brought me to the ship. The infant's skin was more of a dark clay color; the head and eyes were very large. It was covered in some type of clear skin-like membrane and did not look happy or healthy.

"The man with me told me the infant represented the new generation of hybrid beings but that some type of virus was killing them and they were desperate to find a cure. He also told me that the Travelers themselves were reduced in numbers and were trying to survive, but the future looked grim. He said they were hoping to create a hybrid being capable of living in our society—the only way they could continue their threatened species—but their plan wasn't working. He told me there were other powerful forces in the universe that were determined to kill off the Travelers and all their offspring.

"He also said that a secret group within the US government is also at work trying to capture the technology the Travelers offer, but because the Travelers wouldn't cooperate, the secret group is trying to wipe their entire race out and steal whatever they can. The hybrid man quickly added that a secret part of the United States government recently made a deal with the hostile aliens and agreed to help them destroy the Travelers in exchange for their technology.

"Suddenly, the being that brought me there was standing by my side. He told me it was time for me to leave. He said I wouldn't remember everything I was shown, and that it was for their protection. As he brought me back into the elevator room, he promised me he'd come back for me in the future. A second later, I found myself back in bed—it was eight in the morning. I felt very tired and had a bad head-ache. Was it a dream? I don't believe so; everything was as real as me talking to you now. As the day went on, I started to forget what had taken place, like it was disappearing from my mind. I thought I'd write down what I could remember while it was still with me."

The contacts didn't end here; like the Travelers promised, the man would have a number of experiences that have continued up to this book's publication. In winter 2008, he phoned me and related an abduction experience that happened while he was wide awake. His abductors weren't the Travelers, however, but a much different, more hostile race.

"I was lying in bed and it was late at night. I'm not sure of the exact time, but it was well after midnight. I heard a sound close by and tried to open my eyes and move, but I was paralyzed. I finally managed to open my eyes and saw that I was not in my bedroom, but on a table in a very dark room. To my right was an alien being moving his hands and arms as if he was doing something to me.

"He looked a little different than the Travelers from my other experiences. This being was dark gray and very thin with a large, almost pear-shaped head. He had elongated, yellow eyes. I was pretty scared because this thing looked more like a praying mantis than anything else. It was very short and the edge of the table was up to the lower part of its chest. It didn't seem to be wearing any clothes and lacked the physical features of a male and/or female.

"With a mighty burst of energy, I fought the paralysis, broke the creature's hold on me, and jumped up. The creature was very surprised when I did this, reacting like it wasn't supposed to happen. I grabbed it by its neck, surprised at how fragile it was and that its skin felt like cold rubber. I carried it into another room and saw a woman lying on a table also apparently paralyzed. I called out to her, asking if she was okay. This woman turned her head and screamed when she saw me carrying this creature. Then I heard a voice in my head. Whoever it was wasn't talking to me but to the creature I was holding by the throat. It said, 'You picked the wrong one to take. He is protected and genetically sealed and dangerous to us.' Then there was a flash of light and I found myself sitting in my bed in my room. I must have been transported back somehow. I was awake the entire time—this was no dream!"

It's obvious from the report above that there is more than one species abducting human beings—perhaps they're in some type of conflict with each other. If this was just one isolated incident, we could dismiss it as a dream or the result of an overactive imagination. However, this case is not isolated: people across the country and world are having similar experiences.

## The Aliens from the Pleiades

The next case study came to my attention in 1994. It involves a woman named Laura, who since childhood, has experienced a great deal of paranormal phenomena. When Laura was only five years old, she had an "imaginary friend" who lived in the wall of her room.[1] She would talk to her friend and faithfully leave food every night that was always gone by morning. She thought for sure that her friend came out of the wall late at night and ate the food. As an adult, Laura thinks it was strange that her mother never told her to stop leaving food in a dish near the wall. When she was older, she asked her mother about the food, but she seemed to have no knowledge of Laura's childhood habit.

Throughout her childhood, Laura would wake up in the middle of the night and see strange beings she called "witches" enter her room. These "witches" were very tall and skinny with long faces and dark eyes. They had the ability to disappear into thin air whenever Laura's mother came running in the room after hearing her scream. Beginning when she was five years old, the beings would enter her room from the closet area at least two to three times a week. Many times, she was unable to move and would have the feeling of being taken to some other place outside her home. However, Laura has little conscious recollection of what took place when she was taken.

The earliest UFO sighting she can remember happened when she was nine years old. Laura and her friends were

---

1 I've spoken with quite a few UFO abductees who, as children, had an imaginary friend. To them, the "friend" was not always human but engaged the child in conversation, especially at night. According to researchers at the University of Manchester, it has been theorized that children with imaginary companions may develop language skills and retain knowledge faster than children without them. (Source: "Imaginary Friendships Could Boost Child Development." *Science Daily,* Mar. 9, 2005.)

playing on a dead-end street when a large UFO appeared out of nowhere, hovering over the trees. Although her friends ran home screaming, Laura stood and watched the object and was later joined by her mother. Both mother and daughter watched the object for about a half hour. Laura had no fear of the UFO—she had a feeling that it was there to take her home. She still remembers the sighting vividly to this day. She described the object as being a very large disc shape with a series of white blinking lights on the bottom. Due to the time of year and the available daylight at the time, she was able to make out the underside as smooth and silver in color. After the half hour had passed, the object shot straight up into the sky and without a sound, disappeared above the clouds.

When Laura was ten, she had her tonsils removed. She wasn't afraid of the hospital, but once they put her on the operating table on her back, looking up at the bright lights, she was terrified. To this day, bright lights placed above her head make her feel very uneasy. There is no doubt Laura is subconsciously remembering some aspects of her many abductions, a common theme in these kinds of cases being the bright lights and being laid on a table.

Since experiencing these nighttime visitations, Laura has found it difficult to sleep. As an adult, Laura will only sleep three to four hours a night, still fearful that the creatures will come back for her. When Laura does manage to sleep, a multitude of images enter her mind. In one of these visions, she saw a plane crash and saw identification numbers on the aircraft as it fell from the sky. Within a day or so of the plane crash dream, the news carried a story about a crashed plane—the identification number matched the one in her dream. Laura finds this type of experience frustrating and disheartening; she knows something terrible will happen but is powerless to stop it. Recently, Laura has also developed a talent for finding lost items and missing people. Psychic ability is one of several common threads I have noticed in the contact phenomenon. Alien intelligence seems to be very interested in people with psychic abilities and might be keeping them under some type of close surveillance. Laura is now in her early fifties and contact with this alien intelligence seems to be increasing.

Like most people who have contact experiences, she has been plagued with all types of electromagnetic disturbances. On more than one occasion, all the clocks in her house have stopped at 3:15 AM. I found this very interesting because the majority of paranormal cases classified as "high strangeness" take place between two and four in the morning.[2]

As an adult, Laura has continued to have UFO sightings.[3] While driving home on I-84 in Newburgh, New York, in 1982, Laura, her husband, and two children were shocked to see an immense triangle-shaped UFO appear out of the clouds. It

---

2 "High strangeness" is term coined by the late Dr. J. Allen Hynek to describe UFO cases that have a number of paranormal events attached to them.

3 Laura witnessed the Hudson Valley UFO. During a period from 1982–1985 thousands of people in New York and Connecticut reported a close encounter with a giant triangular UFO. These sightings are documented in my book *Night Siege: The Hudson Valley UFO Sightings*.

was about 9 PM on a summer evening and the sky was quite dark. The family pulled over to the side of the highway, and Laura and her two children got out of the car. Her husband did not come out—he sat in the car, almost unresponsive to what was taking place. Laura told me he looked like he was in some type of trance. As they watched the UFO, they realized it was very low in the sky and that there was some sort of cloud around it. They were right under the UFO, and she told me it was so huge it looked like "a floating city." They could see frosted windows around the craft, and inside the windows, Laura saw shadows moving around. The huge ship made no noise and appeared to be composed of a silver-gray metal. As they watched, a beam of blue light shot down from the object just off to the left and right of where they were standing. Suddenly, two smaller ships about one-tenth the size of the larger one came out of nowhere and did three circles around the big ship. The smaller objects were also triangular in shape and had blue and green lights. The large ship then ascended slowly and the smaller ones followed.

After this sighting, Laura and her family began to experience a great deal of unusual phenomena, including poltergeist activity in their home and a number of abductions by an unknown alien intelligence.

The paranormal activity (in particular, the abductions) tormented her so much that she desperately searched for help. She was told of a Native American shaman in Arizona who understood her situation and how to deal with it. So, in the late eighties, Laura traveled to meet with him. What took place is one of the most unusual stories I have ever heard in all my years of paranormal investigation.

The shaman, who was referred to as "Jade," told her she would have to go through a special ritual called "soul retrieval."[4] Jade felt the alien beings had stolen a part of Laura's life force. He told her they must both leave their bodies and confront these entities to bargain for the return of her soul.

As the ritual began, Jade tied a rope around Laura's waist and took her hand, warning her not to let go—he felt the beings were very powerful and that confronting them would not be an easy task. In a guided trance, they left their bodies, and Laura tells me she remembers flying through the sky, holding on to Jade. They traveled and passed through a door that led them to a ship. There, they found three beings standing in a room. The beings were hairless, quite tall, and had long arms, round heads, and pointy chins. Laura says they seemed to be covered in a silvery glow that gave them a very nonhuman appearance. Laura said the shape of their heads reminded her of the "witches" who came into her room at night when she was a child. As she stood there in awe, Jade seemed to be in an argument with the beings to return a part of Laura, a part they'd had in their possession since she was a child. The beings said they were from the Pleiades and have been with Laura's family for generations. They explained that they needed her life force because it gave them the energy they needed to live. They also said

4 Soul retrieval is a shamanic New Age practice that attempts to recover a body's disconnected soul. It's believed that the soul may leave or become fragmented in times of mental or physical trauma or illness.

they had been in contact with Laura's grandmother and mother, and were also beginning contact with her daughter.

When Laura was younger, she had a miscarriage, and the beings told her that baby didn't die—they had it now because it belongs to them. Just then, a human-looking woman brought out a baby for her to see. She thought it was the one she had lost, but the child was much too young. The baby looked almost human, but upon closer examination, more closely resembled the beings in the room. The woman-alien told Laura it was her child and for years had been in "stasis" until the time was right for the child to "grow." The woman escorted Laura further into the ship, to a large, brightly lit, oval room. It was filled from top to bottom with rows of cylindrical canisters, each full of a bubbling liquid containing a fetus. All the infants appeared to be of similar age.

Laura opened her eyes and was suddenly back in her body, remembering every part of her ordeal. The shaman told her that in all of his years helping people, he had never been aboard a ship. As for the ritual, it seemed to have been in vain—when Laura returned home, the strange light and being sightings continued.

As mentioned earlier, Laura's daughter, "Stacy," seems to be part of this contact experience. When Stacy was very young, she was unusually inquisitive for her age: while other kids were more concerned with the ice cream flavor of the month and hanging out at the mall, she was more interested in reading books on different religions and philosophy. From her early childhood days to her adult life, Stacy has also claimed to be in some type of mental contact with a female entity she refers to as "Troy." Troy has told Stacy she has been chosen for a special purpose, and although there are many things that may seem bad in her life now, her situation will only improve. Like other women of her family in pervious generations, it's clear that Stacy is next in line for contact with these beings who say they are from the Pleiades.

## They Come Through the Walls at Night

I received many calls, letters, and emails concerning UFO sightings and contact experiences from 1984 to 2005. A very high percentage of these reports came from the towns of Ellenville and Pine Bush in New York, located on the west side of the Hudson River. The area has always been a rich source of tales and folklore telling of small, human-like beings roaming the hills, dating as far back as the seventeenth century. It's no wonder the author Washington Irving selected this location for his classic short story "Rip Van Winkle."[5] I've conducted a considerable amount of research in the area and was familiar with the paranormal phenomena taking place, especially in Pine Bush. Hundreds of people were frequently gathering to share their experiences at a "Town Hall" type of meeting. On more than one occasion, I attended these get-togethers to hear credible people come forward and speak

---

5 "Rip Van Winkle" was written by Washington Irving in 1819. The story centers on a lazy man who walks up into the hills and encounters strange, small beings. He then falls asleep and wakes up twenty years later to find many things changed. After writing this story, Irving admitted he hadn't been to the Catskill area of New York, but had heard legends about a race of gnome-like creatures that lived in the mountains.

about their very incredible experiences. Besides the dozens of UFO encounters, some people said they had been abducted by aliens more than once in the middle of the night. Out of the fourteen abduction cases I was able to investigate from the Pine Bush area, one stands out for its sincerity on behalf of the abductee, and the interesting fact that more than one family member has also been "taken" by the same intelligence. It is my opinion their experiences were very real (at least in their minds). If they were just making things up and creating a hoax, well, then all of them missed their calling in life and they should have been actors!

It's very rare to find an abduction experience that involves an entire family living together under one roof. This investigation was the result of a number of visits and hours of taped interviews. To give readers a good, but brief, understanding of this case, I will present a detailed synopsis below.

The family in question are residents of Pine Bush and have lived there all their lives. The nighttime visitations from the unknown alien intelligence didn't begin until after the sightings of the giant, dark, triangular object known today as the Hudson Valley UFO, independently witnessed by hundreds. The family members consist of a couple in their thirties and two teenaged daughters, ages fifteen and eighteen. The entire family had seen the unknown object a total of five times between 1983 and 1990, but the sixth sighting was different because that time, the UFO hovered above their home, showing a definite interest in them.

On October 30, 1990, the family had just finished their dinner when they received a call from an excited neighbor telling them to go outside because a UFO was headed in their direction. At first they thought it was a pre-Halloween prank, but the neighbor swore up and down there was something out there, so they all ran outside to the front porch. They looked toward the east end of town and saw a large half-circle of white lights approaching at an altitude they thought was less than a thousand feet. It took only a moment or so for all of them to realize that *this* was the UFO they and many others had seen so many times before. As the object approached, it slowed down and stopped right over their home, after which all four family members heard a buzzing sound. As they looked up and watched the UFO, a brilliant beam of green light projected from the underside of the object, briefly engulfing them. After being "flashed," the light shut off and the UFO continued on its westerly course, moving very slowly like it didn't care who saw it. None of the family members seemed to have any ill effects from the light, and after an excited discussion with several neighbors, they decided to head back inside. As they made their way to the front door, one neighbor yelled out, "I don't want to scare you, but it seemed like the ship was interested in you guys." No one took the comment seriously at the time, but that was to change.

Four days later, each family member felt uneasy, like something bad was about to happen. The house they live in has three bedrooms: one for the couple, and one for each daughter. At approximately two or three in the morning, the couple woke up to a humming sound in the room that seemed to be coming from the bedroom's large walk-in closet. The closet door was open, and they could see a soft green glow illuminating the left side of the wall. Then, six small creatures walked through the wall as if it was liquid, entering the bedroom. The father attempted to get out of bed and confront the creatures, but realized he couldn't move his arms or legs. His wife also suffered the same strange paralysis. The creatures moved toward them and at that moment, just before both of them blacked out, they heard both daughters scream. The next thing they remember was their bedside clock reading 5:17 in the morning. Without saying a word to each other, the husband and wife jumped out of bed and ran to see if the children were all right. As they approached their bedrooms, both girls came running out, screaming about the "aliens" who came through the wall. They described the aliens as being only three feet tall with dark, scaly skin and large eyes. All agreed that whatever they saw looked like a cross between a human and an insect. During the next six months, the aliens would come through the wall and take all of them twice more. Each time, the incident would happen as if it was a repeat performance of the first time. Not one family member has a conscious recollection of what took place after blacking out. All four now sleep in the same room and have piled up furniture and other things against the bedroom walls. Since they have built this makeshift blockade, the bug-like aliens have not returned. It has been over a year since the last experience; all four people are hoping and praying the creatures are gone for good.

I am still working on this case, but the family believes it was their interest in the UFO that drew the attention of the "aliens" to them in the first place; they don't wish to investigate the case further, for fear of the ship and/or creatures returning. In the summer of 2008, I arranged for the father and mother to undergo hypnosis from a qualified psychologist who has worked with me in the past. Unfortunately, the results of those sessions revealed a number of very personal things involving interactions between the aliens and the family. I am not at liberty to reveal the results at this time, but hope to do so at some point in the future.

## Aluminum Foil and the Aliens

Although I take all my cases seriously, this next one has a humorous tone to it. I firmly believe the person involved has had multiple contacts in his lifetime, but as I've noted in the past, the "aliens" really never explain themselves and the individual involved is left trying to interpret the contact experience. This case came to my attention in 1987. I continued my contact with the witness, Dan, until about 2002. In 2008, I was informed he'd passed away at the age of 84.

Dan was a longtime resident of Bethel, Connecticut. Beginning in the early fifties, he had fostered an interest in the UFO phenomenon, known in those early days as "flying saucers." From 1956 to 1987, Dan had at least ten sightings of objects he couldn't identify and after a while, he began to believe that the space ships he was seeing had a special interest in him. He decided to attempt contact with the aliens and find out all about them. In the mid-eighties, Dan had a large sign made which he placed high on a building close to the center of town for all to see, especially any "aliens" that might be passing over. The sign featured a friendly message that welcomed any "space people" who should happen to visit Bethel.

Dan had a habit of driving out to an isolated cemetery where he would wait for most of the night, in hopes that the "people in the saucers" would come for him. Nothing happened in the many years of these nighttime vigils, but during one of his stakeouts in 1987, an event would take place that would change the way he looked at "flying saucers and space brothers" for the rest of his life.

On June 23, 1987, Dan drove out to the cemetery at ten at night to select an isolated area to park his convertible. The night was moonless, warm, and clear, with a slight wind. As he sat in his car, Dan began to meditate, hoping to make a positive connection with the space people, but as the hours passed, nothing happened. It was one in the morning, and he was ready to give up when he heard a very audible voice from above his head say, "Don't leave yet, my friend. We are coming." He tried to answer the voice and ask who "they" were, though at first he thought the town's older teenagers were playing another prank on him. (They liked to make fun of him, as his interest in aliens and UFOs was well known.) A moment later, his car and the ground around him lit up in a white light that seemed to be coming from above. Dan looked up and saw a triangle-shaped ship, measuring at least fifty feet from end to end. The object was very dark, but had white lights on the bottom part of the apex. "It was just hovering right above me noiselessly, no more than a hundred feet in altitude," he said.

Dan was afraid to move and got a definite feeling the "people aboard the ship" wanted him to stay. Then he heard a hissing sound coming from the gravestones and saw several beings interacting with the graves in some way. The closest one was about fifty feet away and he described it as resembling a giant lizard standing on two legs. The first thought that came to his mind was that the "alien lizard men" were digging up dead bodies for a reason that was definitely not good; all he could think about was the '50s cult film *Plan Nine From Outer Space*.[6] Dan said the lizard aliens on the ground lost interest in the graves and started to walk towards him. He turned on the ignition (thanking God that it worked), and stepped on the gas. He took off without looking back. When he arrived home, he locked the doors, pulled down all the shades, and spent the entire night in the corner of his living room in the dark, hoping the lizard men wouldn't find his house. "The thought that came to my mind was that they wanted to make me into a zombie slave to help with their invasion plans," he recounted.

Luckily, nothing else happened that night, but in the weeks that followed, Dan claimed he was visited by three men dressed in black suits who said they were from the air force and were interested in his experience. Dan told me, "they showed identification and came in this big, black car with government plates on it." Dan believed they had him on a list because he had written many letters to the air force

---

6 *Plan 9 from Outer Space* is a 1959 science fiction/horror film written and directed by the infamous Ed Wood, Jr. The film's plot centers on alien beings who seek to conquer planet Earth. To do so, the aliens implement "plan 9," a scheme to resurrect Earth's dead as zombie minions the aliens can control.

and other agencies concerning his interest and sightings of "flying saucers" over the years. Also, after his experience at the cemetery, Dan called a number of people (including the author) on his home phone to talk about the encounter shortly after it took place. His theory was that "government agents and the men in black" intercepted the calls and were keeping him under surveillance. Dan said, "The men in the black suits told me to be quiet about seeing aliens, as they didn't want to cause a panic. If I had any more sightings in the future, I was to just pick up the phone without dialing and say what happened . . . they said they'd be able to receive my report." The men returned to their car, drove away, and never returned.

Although there were no other UFO reports that night, the Bethel police received complaints from local residents that a number of graves and stones in the cemetery were disturbed and apparently vandalized. The police assumed the culprits were trouble-causing teenagers, but no suspects were ever found. Since the complaints seemed to be of an isolated incident, the police filed the reports away without a second thought.

In the years that followed, Dan didn't have any more sightings or encounters but said he felt he was being watched at night. He told me that although he didn't see any, he knew aliens came into his house at night to take him. Dan had no recollection of being abducted but said he always knew when it happened because the morning after, he would feel "terrible, with a headache and strange marks on [his] body."

Once, Dan asked me how aliens could enter have entered his home—he made sure to shut and lock all the windows and doors. I informed him of a number of cases I'd investigated in which the aliens were able to walk right through an abductee's wall like it was nothing and take the person. In retrospect, I shouldn't have told him that, because afterwards, Dan became so paranoid about the lizard men coming to get him that he started sleeping during the day in order to stay awake all night. He also read in some crazy alien abduction book that the aliens could not come through a house's walls if they were lined with aluminum foil. So, Dan took the "advice" and the inside of his house (luckily he lived alone) resembled a bright mirror. He went and spent thousands of dollars on thin sheets of strip aluminum, ordinarily used in scientific, industrial, and aeronautical applications. He was convinced it was working because afterwards, he started to wake up feeling great, and didn't find any new marks on his body.

When I asked him about the marks on his body and whether he ever photographed them, Dan replied that he did, and showed me several photos of his legs and arms. To me, they only looked like scratches, but who knows for sure?

I didn't hear from him for several months but one day, Dan called me out of the blue expressing concern that the "lizard men" would find a way to penetrate the aluminum shield; he had started digging tunnels in his basement to escape if they ever made it through.

Two days later, I received a call from Dan at five in the morning. He was very upset—he had woken up with a headache and found a weird, red, circular mark on his ankle. He was convinced that the lizard men finally found a way to get into his home and had abducted him. I told Dan it *was* possible that any creature with the technology to travel the stars might eventually find a way through his aluminum shield. Well, that was the wrong thing to say! The next thing I heard was Dan screaming something I couldn't make out, followed by the sound of his phone hitting the floor with a thud. The first thought that came to my mind was, "My god, did I scare him about the mark on his foot? Did I give him a heart attack?!" I was really worried and stayed on the phone, yelling into it, asking if he was all right. Silence. I hung up and started to dial 911. As I was ready to hit the last "1," a car came screeching into my driveway. I walked out the front door and there was Dan (who at the time, lived five minutes away), running at me, yelling, "THEY PUT A PROBE IN ME!" As he was running, Dan was trying to lift up his pant leg in an attempt to show me the mark. In his panic, he fell over twice. I went over to him, helped him up, and asked to see the mark. He lifted up his pant leg. I looked at it and said, ". . . that's not an alien abduction mark. It looks like a mosquito bite." Dan breathed a sigh of relief, and I invited him in for a cup of coffee. We had a long discussion, after which he left for home a little calmer. The truth of it all is that yes, the mark looked more like an insect bite of some kind than anything else, but even if it didn't, I was not going say much more. Dan's passionate interest in the UFO experience had quite plainly become the sum of his fears.

# SIX

# WHEN LEGENDS
# COME ALIVE

Legends of beings from other realms of existence are common around the world. Fantastic creatures such as fairies, gnomes, elves, leprechauns, djinn, and Native American earth spirits are but a few examples. We might be seeing the same thing as our ancestors did today, but instead we call them ghosts, aliens, demons, and interdimensional entities. As "spirits" from other realms, they are able to take shape using cues from the mind of the human they contact, usually a shape that best serves their purpose.

Fairies—especially the djinn and the leprechauns—seem to change shape frequently; one of their favorite forms is that of an animal. The shapeshifting ability of Europe's fairies bears a striking resemblance to the Native American trickster spirits. Despite being incorporeal, these beings seem capable of interacting with us and our reality with little difficulty. Some of the fairy race are said to be kind to people, often the guardians of unspoiled forests, rivers, hills, and mountains.

Other fairies are said to be cruel beings that enjoy tormenting humans who foolishly encroach upon their domain. In their true form they resemble globes of colored light and may be seen in locations where dimensional portals exist. Perhaps the phenomenon known as the "spook light" is some type of fairy-like being that guards the doorway to another dimension, or perhaps fairies are trapped in our world and are trying to find a way home.

Although historical encounters with fairy-like beings are common in most of Europe, I was interested in sightings of them that took place in New York's Hudson River Valley. After doing a considerable amount of research, I found that the Native Americans in the area knew of certain locations considered to be the homes of earth spirits and various forms of tricksters. Written accounts of little people and strange beings on the west side of the Hudson River date to pre-colonial times. A very old legend tells of the crew of the *Halve Maen* (Dutch for "half moon"), Henry Hudson's famous ship, encountering fairy-like entities in New York's Catskill Mountains.

## The Gnomes of the Catskills

On September 11, 1609, Henry Hudson sailed the *Half Moon* into the mouth of a great river which would later be named after him. The explorer and his crew journeyed north for several days, trading with the Iroquois tribe while searching for a northwest passage to China. During one of his many stops, a medicine man warned Hudson to stay out of the hills at night because it was the home of many earth spirits that were able to take the form of men or beasts. The medicine man told Hudson that the spirits of the mountains were known to use magic to take people away or make them fall asleep a very long time. Hudson didn't believe the stories and thought they were just foolish tales used to scare the tribe's children to keep them from venturing into the hills at night. As the *Half Moon* continued its northerly journey, it reached the location that would be later known as Albany. Here, Hudson realized that no such passage to China could exist, so he turned his ship south and sailed back down the river.

That night, the *Half Moon* sailed by the foot of mountains known today as the Catskills. Sometime after midnight, Hudson and his crew were woken up by the sound of music coming from the mountains, echoing through the valley. Taking ten crew members, the *Half Moon* anchored so the curious men could follow the sound deep into the woods. They estimated the sound was coming from a high point in the mountains, and so they prepared to climb. The music grew louder as Hudson and his men climbed higher and higher. As they reached the top of the mountain, they were surprised to see a group of small men no more than four feet tall, with long, bushy beards, large heads, and big round eyes, dancing and singing around a fire.

Hudson realized these must be the beings the medicine man had warned him about earlier. One of the bushy-bearded men spotted the explorers and welcomed them with a friendly cheer. The strange little men surrounded the crew and led them closer to the fire, where Hudson and his crew, whether by choice or under enchantment, began to dance.

Hudson was delighted with these small people, and found the hard liquor they had brewed to be extremely delicious. Hudson's men drank and played ninepins with the little men long into the night, while Henry drank and chatted with the gnome chief about the mysteries of the universe.

After a long time had passed, Hudson realized it was getting late and the rest of the crew who were waiting on the ship might be worried about them. He looked around for his men, but couldn't find them. All he saw were large groups of gnomes, laughing and joking as they sprawled around the fire. Then, to his astonishment, he recognized several of them as his crewmen! They had undergone a transformation: their heads had swollen to twice their normal size, their eyes were huge and black, and their bodies had shrunk until they were almost half their original height.

Hudson was alarmed, and asked the leader of the gnomes for an explanation. He told Hudson their transformation was due to the magical liquor the gnomes brewed and that it would wear off in the morning. Hudson wasn't sure whether he believed the leader of the little men, and became suddenly afraid of what else might happen to him and his crew if they stayed. Hudson quickly took his leave of the gnomes and hurried his severely drunken crewmen down the mountain and back to the ship. The entire crew slept late into the morning as if they were under the influence of some kind of spell. When they woke, the crewmen who had accompanied Hudson into the mountains resumed their human forms. The crew continued its journey and by October 4, the *Half Moon* reached the mouth of the great river, where it set sail for home.

On September 11, 1629, twenty years to the day that Hudson and his crew met the Catskill gnomes, early settlers in the area reported a bright fire and the sound of wild music floating through the mountains. Legend says that every twenty years, the Catskill gnomes return to our world, spending several nights dancing around a great fire, drinking their magic liquor. At midnight, they are said to be joined by the spirits of Henry Hudson his crew, and together, play ninepins until crack of dawn. Each time a player rolls a ball, a peal of thunder shakes the mountains, and the fire flares up like bolts of lightning into the night sky. The revelry lasts until daybreak, at which hour the spirits of the sailors depart from our world, promising to return.

During the Dutch settlement from 1650 to 1709, hunters who ventured into the Catskills at night claimed to have seen the spirits of Hudson and his crew drinking, dancing, and playing ninepins with the gnomes. Legend says that any man foolish enough to drink the gnomes' magic liquor would sleep from the moment the spirits departed the mountain to the day they returned, twenty years later. It was this tale that inspired Washington Irving to write his classic story "Rip Van Winkle." In modern times, every twenty years in September and October, people in the area still report hearing mysterious sounds of thunder and phantom music. At night, some claim to have seen ghostly lights and fires on the highest peaks. Some say they're UFOs, but the old-timers claim they're the ghosts of Hudson and his crewmen drinking the magic brew and playing ninepins with the gnomes.

### The Leprechaun, the Trickster, and the Djinn

Throughout human history, no other transcendental being has captured the imagination in quite the same way as the mysterious leprechaun. According to most legends, leprechauns are small, mischievous, fairy-like beings that live in Ireland's hills. Believe it or not, beings of similar description have been reported over the past two thousand years in many other countries, known by different names. To the Native Americans they were the tricksters who had magical powers and the ability to shapeshift. The tricksters delighted in playing pranks on humans and though they were sometimes characterized as playful children, they were notoriously capricious, capable of turning into angry, malevolent creatures without cause or warning.

The origins of the word "leprechaun" may come from the Irish word *leipreachán,* meaning "small spirit" or "sprite." The concept of the leprechaun is believe to have come from ancient legends of a race of mythical inhabitants of Ireland who lived there long before the Celts arrived. In several of these myths, the race was punished for unknown reasons, and were banished to another plane of existence. This story is very similar to the Middle Eastern djinn, who are said to have lived on this planet long before humankind. As Earth's first inhabitants, the djinn became very corrupt and used their powers to destroy rather than create. As a result, a higher order of being (angels) took them out of this world and placed them in a parallel world close to our own. Like the djinn, a leprechaun will grant you three wishes if you make a deal with it, capture it, or help it in some way (e.g., if it's ensnared somehow). But be warned—they are tricksters! According to legend, any favors or wishes granted always turn out for the worst, leaving you with your last wish as: "I wish I never wished for anything at all!" *"Three wishes I will grant thee, anything big or small . . . but if ye wish a fourth time, I'll take away them all!"*

## The Joker

In addition to fairies, gnomes, and leprechauns, a small humanoid being that has been referred to as the "joker" has been reported in the hills of Ellenville and Putnam Valley. The creature is described as being a foot tall, dressed in red, and having a face like the joker card in a deck of playing cards. The joker-creature has been seen running through the forest on the west side of the Hudson and around the mysterious stone chambers on the east. Out of the nine reports of this creature I've found, the following is one of the most interesting.

The first report centers on an individual who has a history of UFO sightings and at least one abduction, wherein he was taken to a secret underground laboratory in the Hudson Valley area by an alien intelligence. At this underground location, the individual says he was used for genetic experiments and was forced to have sex with an alien-human hybrid female. While resting on the couch in his basement several days later, the man noticed movement by the window. At first, he thought it was a bird, but then something knocked on the glass. He looked up and saw a small human-like figure dressed in red with a white face, green hair, and bright red lips. It paced back and forth and occasionally stopped to watch him sitting on the couch. He was dumbstruck at what he saw, and then without warning, the creature jumped through glass without breaking it and landed on his basement floor. It stopped for a second, looked at him, laughed, and ran up the stairs. The witness ran after it, and as he reached the first floor, his dog also saw the creature and took off after it. The joker-creature quickly went into the bedroom, slid under the bed like a major league baseball player coming into home plate, and vanished. The witness thought the strange being was sent by the aliens that abducted him to keep an eye on him. Although the individual's encounters with the aliens and the UFOs continued, the "joker" never returned.

### The Leprechauns of the Stone Chambers

When you think of leprechauns, Ireland's rolling hills probably come to mind, but would you believe these creatures are not restricted to that country? They've been spotted in North America, in New York state, on several occasions. Their favorite hangout seems to be in and around the stone chambers, themselves thought to be of Celtic or pre-Celtic origin.

The stone chambers of New York's Hudson Valley are the locations of a great many unexplainable occurrences ranging from UFOs to ghosts. Over the past twenty years, people who hike in the Putnam Valley area near one of these stone chambers have reported seeing a little man about twelve to fifteen inches tall, running in and out of the entrance of several of these stone structures.

*The stone chamber called the "King's Chamber" in Putnam Valley, New York. Is this the home of the little man of the woods? (Photo credit: author)*

In a recent incident (summer 2005), while hiking in Fahnestock Park at the location of the "King's Chamber," one witness saw something running out of its entrance. At first he thought it was a rabbit, but he realized it was standing upright and resembled a little man. The hiker began to chase the "little man" through the woods and was able to get a good look at it before it jumped into a deep pit. He described it as being a foot tall, dressed in a red, one-piece, skin-tight leather suit with green boots. What really shook the hiker up was that before the creature dove into the pit, it stopped, looked at him, and laughed. He described its face as being pale white with large eyes, and long, orange hair streaked with green.

Shortly after the sighting, I went out to the location where the hiker had seen the "little man" and found the pit he'd jumped into. The pit seemed to be about thirty feet deep and was partially flooded. I had heard about numerous pits in the area connecting with a vast network of underground passages. Some local historians believe that they were dug by Dutch settlers in the seventeenth century as ventilation shafts for a mining operation, and others say they were dug by the Native Americans and used as meditation or burial holes. No one truly knows their origin, however, because no records of who actually dug them or what purpose they served exist. As I examined the pit, it was clear to me it would have to be explored. Soon after, I returned to the pit with a fellow researcher, armed with the proper equipment to descend into this dark hole, which, according to the local Wappinger tribe, is the home of a trickster who protects the forest.

### Into the Trickster's Lair

My friend and I arrived at the pit at nine in the morning in late September. The air was cool, the sky was cloudless and blue, and it looked like it was going to be a perfect day. The opening to the shaft was about six feet across, more than enough room for me to fit. My companion stayed behind, just in case I got into trouble.

The first task was to measure the distance down to the water. I was relieved to find that it was only thirty-four feet; we had more than enough rope. My main concern was the water's depth, as I really didn't want to have to swim in that cold, dark, murky underground pit. If the water was too deep, we would have had to return with an inflatable raft. How did I know my way around the pit/mine shaft so well? In the mid- to late '90s, I'd explored the lost mines of Putnam county with my investigative partner that day, Marianne

Horrigan. The adventures proved to be pretty dangerous, but they prepared me well for climbing into the pit. I put on rubber waders, similar to ones fly fishermen use, hoping it would keep me dry me from my feet to my chest.

I lowered myself down the rope, armed only with an aluminum pole, a camera, and a flashlight. I reached the water level and slowly submerged. I was relieved when I hit bottom: the water was about one meter deep, but that was no guarantee that it wouldn't get deeper in another part of what was looking more like an artificial cavern. I had plenty of extra rope, so I tied it around my waist and slowly walked forward, probing the ground ahead of me with the aluminum rod. I shined the light ahead and was quite surprised to see symbols of some sort, done in white paint. I continued my walk down the dark passage and noticed piles of what seemed like the bones of small animals and birds along the rocks on the eastern wall. Some of the animal remains seemed to be very recent, while others were much older, almost as if they had been there for a very long time. The bones' presence indicated to me that some carnivorous creature lived down there at one time.

I continued my journey down the dark corridor, still carefully probing the ground ahead of me, when suddenly the rod sank down without hitting bottom. Apparently, a large shaft was ahead, and I had no idea how wide or deep this drop was—and didn't want to find out. I slowly turned around and made my way back to the opening, about seventy-five feet away. While walking, I heard a sound behind me as if something large was splashing in the water, heading right for me.

I shined my light into the dark tunnel, but couldn't see anything. I flashed back to the hundreds of science fiction movies I had seen in my younger days, and thought, "Well, this is how the movie always begins—some idiot explores a dangerous area he shouldn't be in, waking up some hungry, prehistoric monster, only to become its lunch." The sound seemed to be getting louder as it echoed off the walls, but luckily, I reached the opening and climbed out quickly. Once back on *terra firma*, my companion and I projected our lights into the hole, but we didn't see or hear anything. Was it just my imagination, or was there some kind of living creature down there, watching and waiting for me to stumble?

In 2006, the New York park rangers filled up the pit with dirt and concrete; the state was afraid someone would fall in and get injured or even killed. Since the pit has been sealed, the strange little joker man or whatever it was has never been seen again.

Is the little man of the pit actually a North American leprechaun? My theory is that gnomes, leprechauns, fairies, and other similar beings are djinn children having a little fun with us unsuspecting humans. The djinn play an important part in the contact phenomenon and paranormal activity manifestations. At present, I am preparing a new book that unveils this strange race of beings who have remained hidden from humankind for thousands of years.

## Bigfoot in the Catskills

To close this chapter, I'd like to mention that fairy and alien beings are not the only strange creatures sighted in the hills of New York—there are also Bigfoot reports that date back more than a hundred years. In my last book, *Files from the Edge*, I explained my belief that Bigfoot and other similar monster-like entities come from a parallel reality very close to our own. These strange and often scary creatures seem to selectively interact with our world and disappear. How or why they do this is unknown, but it would explain their phantasmic nature. Recently, a sighting took place in July of 2008 and was reported by a local newspaper. Although the story was very short and lacked detail, it indicated that unexplainable, strange creatures are still being seen in the Catskill Mountains.

One area resident said she first saw a Bigfoot on her property in March of 2008. She said the creature was near the tree line by her pigpen. "It had a juvenile with it that was about my height," she recalled. The creatures went into the pen and ate her pigs' food but didn't bother the animals.

In another recent sighting, another witness said she had gone to get coffee with a friend one evening and saw a Bigfoot standing along her driveway. She said the creature's eyes were glowing yellow and that she knew it wasn't a bear because it was at least seven feet tall and stood upright like a man. The creature saw her and ran into the woods. She picked up a rock, and threw it near where she believed it was hiding, and something threw the rock back. After a minute she threw a football lying on the lawn, and something threw it back, but very forcefully. Several residents in the area have also claimed to have seen a large, hairy, ape-like animal in the woods.

Strange creatures of time and space have been reported throughout human history and are still being spotted today. Although contact with these creatures seems to be very limited, they are contact experiences nevertheless. A number of researchers who don't accept the multidimensional theory believe that many of the creatures mentioned above—especially Bigfoot—are remnants from a very ancient time, on their way to extinction. I don't agree with this and would be very surprised if these creatures had survived multiple geological epochs, not to mention the threat of urbanization that causes endangerment (and extinction) for so many other species. If the interdimensional theory is discounted, how else could one explain the elusive nature of these entities? When observed, gnomes, leprechaun-like beings, fairies, and even Bigfoot seem like solid beings that often vanish into thin air, leaving behind footprints as the only evidence. These creatures can be photographed sometimes, but more often they don't appear clearly, if at all. The next chapter discusses the entrance and exit points of these otherworldly visitors. There are doorways, portals, and windows that lead to a world we once thought only existed in our dreams . . . or perhaps our nightmares.

# SEVEN

# PORTALS TO ANOTHER DIMENSION

There are several places on Earth that seem to serve as portals to other dimensions adjacent to our own. It's in these places where a great deal of unusual phenomena take place—definitely things we don't consider part of our reality. Such places include the Hudson River Valley in New York, the Bridgewater Triangle in southwestern Massachusetts, the Bermuda Triangle, Stonehenge, and many more locations scattered around the world. The locations I've mentioned above are not randomly placed; they are in fact located on nodes or twisting points in our planet's magnetic field. Although I'd very much like to get into the physics and theory of this idea, that's not this book's purpose. To give you a basic idea of a magnetic node, imagine two shoelaces lying side by side. Each lace represents a line of force that lies parallel to the other. Now, if you take both laces and tie them together to make one loop, you have an area where lines of force overlap, creating greater intensity in the magnetic field. Areas that contain multiple lines of force ("shoelaces") might be the locations in which a dimensional rift or portal could open. When you pull the two strings, the opening or hole forms the loop. The area around the loop will show an increase in the local magnetic field, creating a positive magnetic anomaly. However, the center of the hole that forms the loop will have a much lower magnetic field, creating a negative magnetic anomaly. Note that if you pull the strings too tightly, the opening (the portal) closes. It is my belief that areas of negative magnetic anomalies (decreases in the magnetic field) are where dimensional portals are most likely found. My research has verified this—I was able to take readings with a magnetometer of locations where a great deal of paranormal phenomena had taken place. As I hypothesized, these areas showed a considerable drop in the Earth's magnetic charge.

The area around the loop seems to create a vortex-like effect, causing the center of the loop to have a much smaller field than the surrounding area. The effect is much like a sink filled with water that funnels down the drain when unplugged, creating a small vortex. If you're careful, you can put your finger in the vortex and not get it wet. It is my opinion that this vortical behavior is what takes place in areas of negative magnetic anomalies. The places on our planet that have this special magnetic anomaly might be numerous, and could be the origin of much interdimensional contact.

I would like to present two particular areas in the northeastern United States that have histories of paranormal phenomena, where contact with a variety of entities has taken place with multiple witnesses. The first is Ninham Mountain, located in the Hudson Valley, and the second is the Bridgewater Triangle in southeastern Massachusetts.

## Ninham Mountain

Ninham Mountain is the highest point in New York's Putnam County. From its 1600-foot-high peak, you can see most of Putnam, Westchester, and Dutchess counties. It is a domed mountain composed of many types of granite and a great number of minerals, including quartz, feldspar, garnet, mica, and magnetite. The mountain is named after Daniel Ninham, the last great Native American chief of the local Wappinger tribe. The mountain was important to them, considered a sacred place where the spirits connected with our world. As recently as the last century, shamans would climb to the mountain's top to meditate and enter trances to meet with the spirits of light that lived there. Because it's the highest point in the area, today's state police and federal government have built an antenna "farm" on Ninham's peak, transmitting communication between all law enforcement agencies throughout the southern part of New York. Also on top of the mountain is a ranger tower that is over 100 feet high. The view from the tower is truly amazing; you can see the entire Hudson River Valley from this vantage point.

In *Files from the Edge,* I mentioned Native American ghost sightings reported by hikers on Ninham Mountain. Although I've personally had several experiences at Ninham that could be labeled paranormal, they pale in comparison to what others have reported. The mountain is said to be haunted by

Native American spirits, including Daniel Ninham. On a 1992 hiking trip up the trail, two friends and I heard Native American drumming and chanting that lasted for about ten minutes and then faded away. Recently, in 2009, while filming at Ninham for the Paranormal Television Network (PTN), our crew heard a good ten minutes' worth of Native American drumming that, while not very loud, was definitely audible. Everyone present heard it plainly, but as far as I know, it didn't record on the sound equipment.

### First Encounter

I first became interested in Ninham Mountain in my early days of investigating the UFO sightings in the Hudson River Valley, sometime in winter of 1984. My investigation team was looking for a high vantage point to set up cameras and radio equipment; we wanted to try and document some of the sightings that had been taking place. A resident of Carmel, a nearby town, contacted me to tell us about the ranger tower on top of the mountain and how it would be a great spot to set up an observation post; I could keep surveillance on several counties at once. The first time I visited Ninham was in July of 1985. I was able to drive my car about halfway up the mountain road but then had to park and walk—the rest of the journey was a winding dirt trail that cut into a heavily forested area. On my walk up to the top, I noticed a stone wall off to the right that ended in a small clearing. At first it appeared to be a mound of stones overgrown with thick vines and shrubs. I took a closer look and realized it was a stone chamber, hidden by ages of overgrowth. I cleared away the vines and confirmed that it was indeed one of these structures whose builders remain a mystery. This was the sixth time I had come across one of these chambers in a location known to have a great deal of paranormal activity, UFO sightings in particular. But I digress: my main objective that day was to get to the top of the mountain, climb the tower, and try to document anything unusual that night in the sky. It was getting dark, so the mysterious chamber would have to wait for another day.[1]

I reached the top of the mountain at sunset and began to climb the tall tower—the view was fantastic! At about midnight, the wind picked up and the tower actually swayed back and forth. Although it was July, the windchill at the top made the air feel quite cold. While I didn't observe anything strange in the sky that night, something was definitely happening on the ground, unbeknownst to me.

At 2 AM, I climbed down the tower stairs and made my way down the dark mountain path to the parking lot. I had a strange and uneasy feeling, like something or someone in the woods was watching me. As I continued my walk down the trail, I suddenly heard an audible buzzing sound, followed by a *crack!*. This sound repeated over and over again in fifteen-second intervals. The "crack" sounded as if someone was walking in the woods, stepping on twigs and snapping them. I stopped at the same chamber I'd visited earlier

---

1 A more detailed study of the stone chambers and their connection with the paranormal is presented in my book *Interdimensional Universe: The New Science of UFOs, Paranormal Phenomena and Otherdimensional Beings.* Woodbury, MN: Llewellyn, 2008.

and saw what appeared to be flashes of light. They stayed close to the ground on the right side of the trail, perhaps two hundred yards into the woods. Then, the same thing appeared on the left side of the trail at about the same distance. The activity looked like the light of a camera flash, but the strange thing was that the flashes on the right were bluish-white, while the flashes on the left were yellow. The lights were about as bright as lightning flashes and looked like some type of electrical or plasma discharge. I walked into the woods to my right to see if the source of this phenomenon could be discovered, but I couldn't ever seem to get close enough to the flashes. The closer I got, the further away they seemed to move. I thought to myself that perhaps the light source was actually a great deal further than I had originally estimated. If that was indeed the case, the amount of energy needed to produce the burst I was seeing had to be considerable. The flashes didn't seem to be radiating from one particular point, but appeared to be coming from all directions. Every time the lights flashed, the trees would light up and the trail which was once dark became illuminated. I decided to return to the main trail, when suddenly I began to feel very light-headed and dizzy. I stopped, sat on a rock for a moment, and noticed the flashes of light slowly fade and vanish. Once the flashes disappeared, I felt better and was able to walk to my car. I went home feeling mystified about what had happened that night but guessed it was some type of electromagnetic phenomena. What I witnessed intrigued me so much, I began conducting research on the mountain's history and geology.

## *UFO Encounters*

Ninham Mountain has an intriguing history of UFO sightings. Strange lights that circle the mountain have been seen on many occasions, and some witnesses have even reported large clusters of brilliant, colorful globes settling down on its summit. A restaurant owner in the area reported that she frequently saw lights of various colors circle the mountain. The description of these lights is almost identical to what the native shamans experienced eighty years or so ago. The Native Americans called them the "spirits of the mountain," but local residents today call them "UFOs." Perhaps the most interesting close encounter with the spirit lights of Ninham was that of a forty-eight-year-old man who often visited the mountain for hunting and camping. Following is his story as told to me in 1992. The man is a former government agency intelligence officer we'll refer to as "Thatcher."

### RESCUED BY THE MOUNTAIN SPIRITS

"I was up at Ninham Mountain in January of 1990, doing a little hunting and walking through the woods. I reached the top of the mountain and the wind was gusting really hard; I bet the windchill factor was at least twenty below zero. I was on the north side of the forest when it started to snow. I was already very cold and with the sun gone, the temperature began to drop even more. The wind also started to gust and I could feel my hands, feet, and face starting to develop frostbite. It then began snowing so hard I couldn't see even ten feet in front of me. I quickly became disoriented and could barely move. I knew I was pretty high up; there was nothing around to really shelter me from the wind, as most of the trees were bare. The sky was very dark and there was a fog all around me, the fog was so thick that it was difficult to see and I started to lose my bearings. I felt dizzy, fell to the ground, and couldn't move—it was as if my joints were frozen solid. I thought to myself that this was it; someone would find my frozen body weeks from now. I stopped feeling pain, and knew it was a bad sign. I looked up to the sky and my face became covered with snow. Just then, right overhead, ten or so lights of different colors appeared out of nowhere and started to descend from the clouds, in the shape of a circle. I heard no sound, and it was a very strange thing to see because the lights looked very fuzzy through the mist and fog. Then I blacked out.

"The next thing I remember is waking up in the ranger's station. The ranger told me he found me at the parking area at the bottom of the mountain, lying on the hood of my car. He knew I was there because he'd received a telephone call, alerting them to my dire situation. I have no idea how I got to safety—there was no way I could have walked all that distance on my own. Those lights must have been some sort of ship or maybe a UFO. They must have been friendly because they saved me from a frozen death. It seems that from the point I blacked out until the time that I woke up in the ranger's station was about forty minutes, so it's not like I was missing for days. Whoever my rescuers were, they didn't keep me in their ship for very long. The only thing I remember is being in a room and seeing canisters with figures which looked like people in them. I know this sounds a little crazy, but I remember seeing a canister that was empty and I really felt that whoever they were, they are going to come back for me because that's the canister that I'm supposed to be in."

Thatcher had an interesting UFO experience of some type, and was transported out of danger by an unknown intelligence. This intelligence may also have called the ranger, alerting him to Thatcher's condition. What are the lights of Ninham Mountain? Are they aliens, dimensional entities, or the spirits that guard and protect the mountain? After his experience at Ninham, Thatcher continued to have sightings of UFOs and would hear voices in his head telling him, "You can come with us if you want, but it has to be your choice."

In 2006, I lost touch with Thatcher; his only family member is a sister who said he left a note one day saying not to worry because he was moving away, after which he "vanished off the face of the Earth." I asked some of his friends about him, and they believe he may have moved to another country to hide because he often said that government agents were "after him and wanted to place him in a prison to interrogate him about his alien contacts." Whatever the reason for his vanishing act, it's clear it all began with a contact experience at Ninham Mountain.

## The Bridgewater Triangle

The Bridgewater Triangle is a very large area in southeastern Massachusetts covering an area of more than 160 square miles. Since colonial times, this area has been the site of a great deal of paranormal phenomena, including sightings of giant prehistoric birds; Bigfoot; ghosts and ethereal beings;

and a variety of nonnative, out-of-place creatures. The location is also popular for UFO sightings and mysterious animal mutilations. According to the Native Americans who lived in the area, Bridgewater Triangle was cursed by their ancestors when colonial settlers took over much of their land. Like the stone chambers of New York's Hudson Valley and Ninham Mountain, the Bridgewater Triangle is full of what many believe to be pre-Columbian structures and inscriptions that may date back thousands of years.

One of the most common types of phenomena people have seen in the area is the spook light, sometimes known as a ghost light or will-o'-the-wisp. They look like glowing balls of light and seem to possess intelligence. Spook lights have been known to follow cars and people, but always keep their distance when approached. One of the strangest, most bizarre areas of the Bridgewater Triangle is a place called Hockomock Swamp, which roughly translates to "the dwelling place of the spirits" in Wampanoag. It is here that people have reported encounters with small, humanoid beings that attempt to abduct trespassers. We may never know for sure if the beings have taken anyone; although people have in fact vanished in the area, there is no documentation that the little people of the swamp are responsible. In 2008, Rosemary Ellen Guiley traveled to the swamp and surveyed the area. I admire her actions; that day, a northeastern storm came through and she was out there in very severe weather. Although she didn't see anything out of the ordinary, Rosemary said the place felt very strange to be in. Recently, investigators and residents of the area have reported sightings of black helicopters flying low during the day and night. I have heard many rumors of a secret organization within the government that is attempting to capture an interdimensional being in order to obtain the technology used to "jump" between dimensions. If true, it would explain the otherwise out-of-place military activity in the triangle.

# EIGHT

# EXTRATERRESTRIALS AND ULTRATERRESTRIALS

The study of the human-alien connection is extremely complex because it involves an abductee's psyche, in addition to the possibility of an intelligence that isn't human. The following case involves a young man, Tim, who wrote me in 2008 about alien contact experiences he's had from a very early age. Although his claims may be impossible for many to accept, Tim believes with all his heart, mind, and soul that what has been happening to him is real. To me, Tim's experiences are pieces of the puzzle in the contact phenomenon and should not be ignored. Some of the material Tim sent me has been edited so readers can get a better understanding of his incredible encounters.

## Tim's Story

"My name is Tim. I am eighteen years old, and am about to get my GED. Many people think I'm crazy, or tell me to go to a sanitarium where I can get help. Sometimes, people have been cruel to me and while it's hard to forgive them, I manage, because deep down, I know they don't understand and are scared of the truth. Many people have come to me wanting to know more because they're intrigued. They've said, 'Why did this have to happen to you at such a young age?' My answer is, 'Because there must be more to me than meets the eye.' I have to admit, people have been frightened of me because of what I know. I see a world cowering in the corner, afraid of the truth, because the lie many have lived for so long has become reality and it's all they will accept.

"I believe there's more to God and this multiverse than we can see. I believe the Bible only contains half-truths, left in to confuse the masses and control their minds. I believe that man used religion for mind control, and the complete truth can only be found through guidance from beings and spirits of light, and through combining all of religion's scattered truths. These beings told me about the events of 2012 long before I heard it from the media. I have learned from them that all things share one universal consciousness, the point of all knowledge. As each mind evolves, it becomes more of who we really are and helps us move on to the next higher level.

"I have learned that December 21, 2012, is the end of this cycle for this planet on this physical, galactic plane. Our planet will move to the next dimension, the fifth dimension, and will cease to exist to those still in the third and fourth dimensions. This date will also herald many natural disasters and catastrophes. The effects have only begun, evident in our erratic weather patterns and increased seismic activity. Not only are we looking at geologic and weather changes, geomagnetic changes will also occur. The magnetic poles are going to shift, an event which is long overdue.

"When the poles shift, openings in Earth's magnetic field will form, allowing cosmic and solar radiation to directly affect our planet. Also at this time, the sun will release a coronal mass ejection (also called a CME), causing a third of the earth to be fried, electronics to fail, and many fatalities.

"There are only a few safe areas humans can go for survival. I have been told these locations are marked by crop circles, but only the authentic crop circles, not the hoaxes. Many of the fake crop circles were made by people who like to cause confusion; their fake creations have convinced many that the designs are not a product of an alien intelligence, only human tricksters.

"I have been told that our government has made a pact with a sinister alien intelligence for gaining technological innovations for things like weapons and computers. These evil beings are called Reptilians, and are from a planet called Dracon. The Reptilians are here to stop humans from evolving and wish to exterminate us because we prevent them from ascending. They are carrying out their mission by causing wars and creating disease. I can tell you why Mayan civilization, as great and advanced as it was, is now extinct: they were unable to please the Reptilians. The infamous blood sacrifices Mayans made were really offerings of genetic material to these aliens so they could learn more about our species. Once they had learned everything about the Mayans, they exterminated them, and the Reptilians became the gods of another Earth civilization.

"Another part of the plan is that when the global catastrophe comes, they will have human messengers tell people to go to the false crop circles for safety. When people go to those places, they will be only like lambs being led to the slaughter. Each fake crop circle will have FEMA camps in the vicinity; I was told that more than eight hundred camps will be fully operational, with armed guards, ready to receive prisoners. Despite what we may hope, people will not be able to choose which crop circle in which they will hide because martial law will have been instated and we will lose our basic civil rights.

"I have seen what will happen at these false sanctuaries. People will be forced out of their homes by the military and after they are removed, the area will be destroyed—all who remain will be exterminated without mercy. The people who will be evacuated will be forced to move to a location they will be told is safe, but is not. When they arrive at this location, they will have a choice: submit to slavery and mind control or die.

"These were the visions given to me by the higher-dimensional beings who are trying to save us. The Reptilians are shapeshifters and can take most any form, but I have been told how to identify them. To identify them, one must look into their eyes—Reptilians are incapable of keeping their eyes in one form constantly. Reptilian eyes shift back and forth between human and their original shape. I strongly believe that in my past life, I was one of the alien beings we call the Grays. I was a being of light and chose to come to this planet as a human to help its people. I have a compassion for the people of Earth and want them to know the truth. I understand why people call me crazy—deep down they are scared of change and losing the security they have always known."

### Tim's Experiences as a Child

"When I was ten years old, I remember getting ready for bed, standing in my room and wondering what I should wear to bed. The next thing I knew, it was ten the next morning and I was standing by the window. The next couple of years went by without incidence, but at thirteen, I began to have occasional dreams about events that would come true. My learning process sped up and I was able to understand things much more quickly than most kids my age.

"I had one good friend growing up named Greg. One night, I had a dream in which I was outside in front of a car Greg was driving. He was driving very fast because he was late for something, but suddenly the right front tire blew out, and the car flipped and rolled over. When it stopped flipping and came to a stop, I saw his body hanging three-quarters of the way out of the window; he looked lifeless and was covered in blood. I woke up with a start and thought it was only a nightmare. The next day, I went outside to do my chores and saw Greg drive by very quickly, as if he was in a hurry. Suddenly, the dream flashed into my mind but I pushed it out, thinking I was making things up. Greg never came back. The very next day, my parents brought me the sad news that Greg's car had spun out of control from a blown tire; he was killed in the accident. Right then, my heart sank because I realized I had seen his fate the day before it happened."

## Contact from the Grays in Tim's Dreams

"A few months later, I began having dreams (or what I thought were dreams) of the Grays. They would come to me, asking if I'd take a ride with them. I'd leave with them and travel through the stars and explore the great unknown. In other dreams, I was one of them and part of a crew on a ship. I was happy and we all were connected to each other; everything was peaceful. I woke up crying many times feeling homesick because I wanted to go back with them.

"In November of 2005, I had a dream about going outside to go to our hay barn to get the feed for our horses. When I got to the barn, I felt something there but didn't know what it was until I opened the doors. Inside, I saw one of the gray aliens. I call it a 'him' because there was a masculine energy about him, even though the Grays are physically sexless. To determine their gender, one must sense which energy is dominant.

"We both stood there, staring at each other. I felt a kind of awe that he was there waiting for me. I concentrated on staring into his large, glimmering, slanted black eyes and felt a warm kindness about him. He outstretched his hand, clearly wanting me to take it in mine and when I did, he smiled. I felt an electric energy travel down my arm, whereupon I heard him say telepathically, 'Soon, my brother, very soon, you will know,' and I suddenly woke up. Upon waking, I felt a tingling in my arm much like the feeling in my dream. I went to grab a piece of paper and unbelievably, it stuck to my hand. Then I put my hand by my computer monitor while it was on, and a rainbow appeared (like when it is degaussed). The tingling feeling subsided after a few hours and things returned to normal.

"I tried to put the dream and the strange behavior of my arm out of my mind because the events were causing me great distress; I had no idea what was going on. After meeting the Gray, I began to feel other people's emotions and became hyper-empathic. I began to hear voices and though I didn't know it at the time, someone was trying to telepathically communicate with me. In August 2007, I tried listening to these voices but found it frustrating because they were unclear. One day, while driving on a busy highway, I suddenly heard a loud, clear voice in my head say, 'Move to the right, now.' It sounded urgent, so without hesitation, I trusted the voice and moved over quickly. As soon as I did, a car speeding out of control barely missed me.

"In May of 2008, the Grays showed up again, but this time the encounter was physical."

### The Grays Arrive

"It was at night and I was on my computer when I began to feel a presence. At that moment, I was suddenly transported into the Grays' ship through some type of teleportation.

"The inside of the ship and the room I found myself in was amazing! I saw technology that was manipulated by thought and holographic data that floated through the air. The room was circular and the walls were covered with devices that looked like advanced technology. I looked around and saw the Grays. There were eight of them, each standing at a station monitoring the craft's various systems. They were about six feet tall and their skin was light gray in color. They had strong facial features, and big, black elliptical eyes. As soon as I noticed them, they all turned to face me and gave me a friendly look that made me feel welcome. One of them came towards me and introduced himself as Zantros.

"Everything happening was so incredible that I thought it was a dream, but Zantros told me it wasn't, and neither were the previous contacts. Zantros said I had traveled the stars with them many times via astral projection. He said, 'We come from the Orion constellation; we have come to you because time is getting short on this planet and it is time for you to know what is really going on. You are one of us, and have always been. We were the ones protecting you and were the voices you've been hearing. Your real name is Xzantronos, and you are my son.'

"At this point, tears were rolling down my face because for the first time in my life, I felt like part of something important. While I was on their craft, another Gray caught my eye; this one I knew was female because I could feel the energy. She came to me and introduced herself as Zintron. She said she has been waiting for me for a long time and asked if I desired to take her as a soul mate. Before meeting her, I had given up because I didn't think there was anyone for me in this world. My previous girlfriends had broken up with me because they said I was too complicated. Now I had just met the perfect soul mate—someone who deeply understood me and wanted to be there and care for me and how I feel. Zintron and I decided to deepen our bond, and brought forth a son we named him Orion, after the Orion Constellation. From Earth, when I look at that constellation, I see my home and my son.

"Zantros told me time was limited and that the world I lived in was in danger. He said, 'You are to lead many to the truth and help those who want to ascend.' He then offered me some kind of DNA injection. 'This will assist you with your mental abilities, and help you become more of what you truly are,' he explained. After I let him inject the DNA into me, I immediately felt more aware. I stared into his eyes and felt a deep bond that I believe established a mind link between myself and the Grays. I felt at peace and then we embraced as he said goodbye and told me it was time to leave. I begged them to take me with them; to take me home with them because I felt I didn't belong on Earth. Zantros told me, 'Just a little longer, my son. In 2012, we will come for you and take you home. We need you to help us on Earth right now but we will always be watching over you and will always be in contact with you now. You're not alone anymore, but it's time to go now.' With that, I was transported back into my room and they were gone. I missed them terribly and cried for days, wishing they were here, or I was there.

"Once I was able to come to terms with my grief, I underwent rapid changes; I learned the art of meditation and how to strengthen my link with them. It is now so strong, I no longer have to meditate to contact them or for them to talk to me. They showed me books to read that contain information relevant to my task. The first book they told me to find and read was [the author's book] *Interdimensional Universe*. They told me about this book before I had even heard of it. They tell me which websites are telling the truth, and which videos are real. Because of them, I know who I really am. These beings are our true friends and brothers."

### Another Encounter

"On the night of August 18, 2008, it was raining. I was sleeping when suddenly, a loud clap of thunder roused me half awake. I was about to turn over when suddenly, I felt a hand touch my chest in an affectionate way. When I opened my eyes, Orion was sitting on my bed beside me! I sat up, overjoyed to see him. He looked more Gray than human, but he had my facial structure. We talked for a while about what his home world is like, but after what felt like too little time, he said it was time for him to leave and he teleported back to his home world.

"I have seen their home world with my own eyes because I teleported there by accident while attempting astral projection. When I arrived there, it didn't feel like I was in astral form—I could physically touch things, and breathe the air, which was so sweet and fresh, like how the air once was on Earth. When I materialized, the Grays greeted me warmly and asked if they could help me in any way. The best part of meeting them was that they all knew me like I was an old friend. I asked for a tour of their city, and they were happy to oblige.

"The city I was in had buildings that were tall, about fifty feet, in proportion to each other. An odd thing I noticed was that the buildings were all circular and composed of a material I had never seen before. I looked up and saw the three suns (Orion's belt) in the sky and noticed the deep green of the grass and the bluish tint to the leaves on the trees. I knew immediately this was home. It was explained to me that the Grays live in a society without government; they are all linked together at high psychic and spiritual levels so everyone gets along. Everyone is at peace, doing their own things, free of hate, greed, and other negative emotions. Seeing everyone in such a peaceful society brought tears to my eyes; this is how Earth was supposed to be.

"After the tour, I was brought to my son and mate's home. I stayed there for about three hours, before I realized what time it probably was on Earth. I said my goodbyes and tried to go back but couldn't—I was physically on their planet, not only light years away, but in another dimension. The Grays accompanying me were able to help me return and when I did, it was ten o'clock the next morning and everyone was worried about me. I gave no explanation for my absence; no one would believe me anyway."

———

Tim is still in contact with me and continues to have experiences with a number of different types of aliens. Some of the common threads that I have found with Tim's story and others in my files are the descriptions of the aliens. The image of the aliens as being gray with large heads and big, black eyes is used in popular media in everything from magazines to movies. I have even seen the little guys on pencils, shirts, and lunch boxes. There are also dolls, toys, action figures, and video games featuring this type of alien being. The hit science fiction series *Stargate: SG-1* also used the Grays' likeness in a number of episodes portraying them as a technologically advanced race of beings from another galaxy who wish to save the human race and protect us from the many hostile beings in the universe. Many people feel that large-scale contact will be made very soon and the government has been slowly programming the image of these aliens into our society so when the time comes, the human race will have an easier time accepting them.

## The Silver Lady

I was once told by a well-known UFO investigator that the most serious and dedicated researchers were ones who actually had extraterrestrial contact at some point in their own lives. Although I didn't agree with this sentiment when I first heard it, I think the person who told me this may have been correct, given what I've noticed in my own research and what I've heard from others. The contact experience can happen on many different levels and can involve not only what we call alien beings, but entities from other dimensions. One such researcher who has had a contact experience is Rosemary Ellen Guiley. Rosemary is the most dedicated paranormal researcher I have ever met; she spends a considerable amount of time in the field looking for the truth and trying to understand more about the invisible universe that surrounds us. Rosemary is the author of nearly fifty books on many different paranormal topics and had an interesting experience with a being she refers to as "Silver Lady." Although her experience is considerably different than Tim's, it is still a form of contact with an incredible otherworldly being.

Rosemary's experiences with Silver Lady began with periodic dreams that differed significantly from her normal dreaming pattern. Although her dreams were usually in color, the Silver Lady dreams were in black and white, and the setting was always an unearthly alien landscape.

Rosemary calls the being "Silver Lady" because she appeared in her dreams as a tall woman dressed in flowing, glowing, silver garments. The communication she receives from Silver Lady is not verbal; it is telepathic in nature, and Rosemary notes that Silver Lady usually keeps her face turned away when they meet. Once, when Rosemary was finally able to look upon her face, she didn't see any human features, only an oval swirl of iridescent color like mother-of pearl. This hidden and unusual face is characteristic of encounters with angels and otherdimensional beings.

The purpose of Silver Lady's contact during the dream state is instructional, Rosemary feels, though she can't remember the content upon waking. She does remember seeing images and being shown other worlds where realities exist that differ greatly from Earth's. Reflecting on her dreams, Rosemary believes they were an introduction to the multidimensional nature of consciousness, and to the creative power of thought.

After her revelation, dreams with Silver Lady became more frequent. They were wonderful and full of adventure. The experiences were so positive in nature that when they didn't occur, Rosemary missed them. After having such wonderful experiences, she was sure Silver Lady was an angel.

One night in 1988, Rosemary woke up at about 3 AM to find Silver lady standing beside the bed. She looked solid and glowed with a shimmery, silver light. Her arms were outstretched toward her, and a stream of energy poured through her hands, Rosemary says entered like a data stream flowing into her at great speed. It was as if she was "receiving an upload from a cosmic computer." Information was pouring in so fast that she had difficulty discerning what was what; she had to strain herself physically to absorb it. As the information continued to flow in, Rosemary was powerless to stop it; she was paralyzed flat on the bed but says that during the entire experience, she felt no fear. The "transfer" seemed to last a long time, although in real time it was probably very short. The connection terminated as soon as Rosemary felt she couldn't take any more, and Silver Lady vanished. Rosemary could move again, and she got out of bed feeling somewhat disoriented. She noticed her bedroom window had opened; her belief is that Silver Lady left it open upon her departure as a sign. She closed it, returned to bed, and fell asleep.

Rosemary's interpretation of the information transfer was that it was some kind of blueprint pertaining to her writings and path in life. After the 1988 experience, Silver Lady made no more appearances in her dreams and stopped visiting her at night, to Rosemary's dismay. However, she could still feel her presence.

Then in 1991, Rosemary received a message from Silver Lady through Eddie Burks, a medium and healer who lived in England. Although the message was very long, Rosemary had only one reply: "Who is Silver Lady?" Channeling through Burks, Silver Lady answered: "You do not have quite an accurate picture of me. I am not an angel, but am of the angel realm and the human realm. My function is to be an intermediary between the two worlds for the purpose of interpretation. Seek not to identify me more closely at this stage." The session ended, and Rosemary was satisfied to have finally discovered Silver Lady's identity.

Rosemary and I discussed this contact experience at length, and it was suggested that Silver Lady was perhaps once a physical being who ascended to a higher plane of existence. In some cases, these ascended beings interact with people in our physical realm, although their contact seems to be limited. There are some similarities between the contacts of Dean Fagerstrom's Donestra and Rosemary's Silver Lady. Both seem to be beings that aren't angels, but are from a higher spiritual realm beyond the physical universe. It also seems that both Dean and Rosemary were given information that would guide them on their life paths. There's no doubt that Silver Lady influenced Rosemary and her writings; I have read several of her books and one can easily see the inspiration for her works. Rosemary's website is listed in the back of this book if you'd like to contact her.

## Ongoing Contact with Dimensional Beings

In *Files from the Edge,* I presented the partial experiences of a young man named Bruce. In the book, I explained that there was more to his story—the withheld material was a contact experience and would be included in a new work on the subject. If my readers would like more detailed information on Bruce's early experiences (which apparently served as the catalyst that connected him to another reality), his case study appears in chapter ten, "Messages from Beyond," of the book. A brief synopsis of these early experiences is presented below.

Bruce led a pretty normal life until he and some friends decided to use a Ouija board one night. They just wanted to have some fun and didn't really expect anything out of the ordinary to happen. During the sessions, they were able to contact an intelligence they initially thought was a spirit, but later identified itself as an extraterrestrial. With each session, the communicating entity became more aggressive and unfriendly, demanding control. Although Bruce and his friends stopped using the board completely, this entity—which Bruce described as "evil"—continued to attack him.

Using the Ouija seemed to open Bruce to another reality, setting the stage for a series of interdimensional contacts with many different beings. Bruce believes some of the beings that have contacted him are evil, but he also thinks he's communicated with benevolent beings as well. Bruce gave me his amazing contact story after hearing me speak at the UFO Roundtable Conference in New York. His very complex and detailed story follows.

### Bruce's Strange Experiences

"After using the Ouija board in England and having the problems with evil spirits, the last communication I had with this entity ended with it saying it knew I was going to America, and that it would follow me across the Atlantic. It said I couldn't get away from it and would feel its power. Well, it must have made good on its promise because really strange things happened to me once I arrived in the United States, in 1977.

"I told some friends about everything that happened in England; they were interested and wanted to see a demonstration so they talked me into going to an old cemetery in Washington, Connecticut, where I lived with my parents. We were all just teenagers at the time looking for cheap thrills, so we brought a Ouija board just to see what would happen. We went at night and as soon as we began using it, the pointer began moving and spinning around. Then we heard something that sounded like four or five voices screaming nearby—then it stopped. We used the board again and the noise came back, but this time it sounded like sixty people all yelling something that we could not understand, and we couldn't figure out where it was coming from. It sounded like someone was having a wild party, but the noises were more like growls than people screaming. At times, the noises sounded more animal than human—it was very strange. After a while, the yelling stopped and we left. I guess that in total, we heard those strange sounds for a good twenty-five minutes.

"A few years later, in 1985, one morning at about three o'clock, I suddenly woke up, feeling as if the room was no longer solid . . . like something was opening up somewhere. I heard a voice coming from the basement say, 'You want something.' When I heard the voice, I knew a spirit was in the room with me. It was definitely an evil presence and gave me a horrendous feeling. I couldn't see anything, but I definitely heard noises in the walls and windows. My first thought was that some unearthly being was in the room with me. It felt as if something was trying to get into me by digging down my spine; it was horrible. I couldn't stand it anymore so I left my room, went downstairs to the den, and turned on the television to try to calm myself down, but it didn't work. I sat in a chair and couldn't keep myself from rocking back and forth. I couldn't focus my eyes anywhere for more than a couple of seconds. I felt the thing trying to pull at me and yank my soul out of my body. There were times when I felt taken outside my body and had to force myself back in. It was like a tug of war; something was trying to pull me out and I was trying to stay in. I knew if I could last until dawn, things would be all right and this would be over, at least for a while.

"I knocked on my parents' bedroom door and they saw I was upset. My mother agreed to stay up with me. When we discussed that night years later, my mom said she didn't know what was going on, but she strongly felt that if she hadn't gotten up and sat with me that night, I wouldn't be here today. Morning finally came and I was fine—the evil presence had disappeared.

"The next day I called my friend John, who answered the phone sounding surprised: 'Bruce? Is that you?' I told him that yes, it was me, and asked him why he sounded so shocked. John said he heard me outside his house screaming at four in the morning. When he went outside to investigate, no one was there. He was sure something terrible happened to me but he was afraid to call my house.

"Two weeks later, my cat formed a habit of coming into bed with me. It didn't want to curl up or snuggle, it just stood there, staring at me. After a few minutes of watching me, it would screech, its hair would stand on end, and it would run away. Also around this time, my parents told me I was screaming in my sleep. They said I would yell 'NO, NO, NO, NO!' like I was being attacked. This continued for a while, but I don't really remember anything happening except for a dream I had in which I was walking across a bridge. A being was walking from the other side, approaching me. We met in the middle and looked at each other. When we made eye contact, I suddenly went flying backwards, as if being repelled by a powerful magnetic force. When I was thrown backwards, I 'landed' in my bed and woke up."

### A Visit to Steep Rock, Connecticut

"Life started to return to normal, but it wasn't long before I had what I call interdimensional experiences while hiking through Steep Rock State Park in Washington, Connecticut. I first heard about strange things going on there from a guy named Ned. He told me that years ago, he had a strange vision while hiking at Steep Rock. He had sat down to take a rest, and once he was relaxed, had a vision of the spirit of a man he believed was a Native American chief. The chief's spirit approached him and said Ned had to do something to raise awareness about the race of people that used to live there. Well, much later, a dig was done at Steep Rock and archaeologists discovered that the place where Ned had his vision of the chief was the home of a Native American shaman.

"The area of Steep Rock called Hidden Valley was another place I had more strange experiences. I was there in June of 2008, hiking with my friend Rachel, and I unwittingly took a photograph of something glowing that looked like a fairy, though I didn't see anything in person; the glowing light only appeared on film. We crossed the river (which was only ankle-deep) and I saw something I had never seen before—something I can only describe as a solar waterfall. The phenomenon was very wide, like a waterfall or pillar of sunlight falling from the sky.

"I think my experiences at Steep Rock are related to [the author's] work published in *Interdimensional Universe*. After some traveling, in 1991, I visited the American Indian Institute (near Steep Rock) and purchased a picture of a Native American chief—a very nice picture of a brave, noble-looking person. I hung the picture on my door and left the house. When I came back home, I found a feather on the floor right under the Chief's picture. I picked up the feather and thought it was odd, but didn't dwell on it or read into it too much. When I came home the next day, another feather— a different one—was in the same spot, below the picture. The day after, I wasn't in my room but still in the house and when I went back up to my room, I found yet another feather! What's weird is that this time I was home; I didn't hear or see anything or anyone enter, and have no idea how the feathers got there. It was after this third occurrence that I realized the feathers must have materialized when I wasn't there. I wondered if they were some type of symbol or message, so I said out loud, 'I don't understand what you mean.' When I got home the next day, I found three new feathers under the picture! Six months later, I went up to the attic for something and when I came back down, three feathers had once again found their way below the chief's picture.

"Something must have been triggered, because after I 'asked' the picture and found the feathers, I began to remember unbelievable experiences I'd had at Steep Rock. I thought at first the memories were dreams, but they were incredibly detailed. I was starting to remember a great many otherworldy things that had happened to me that were previously blocked out of my mind. Now, a memory was coming back: I'd had encounters and contact with beings in the Hidden Valley area of Steep Rock. I remember meeting a being there who told me an ancient race once lived there.

"The encounter was in the spring of 1990 when I was hiking with a friend in Steep Rock. After a long journey, we were surprised to meet a very old woman all by herself, except for the goat that was with her. They were standing by the river. I should mention that although the woman looked elderly, there seemed to be an air of power about her. She saw my friend and me, and we went over to her to introduce ourselves. Somehow, she ended up asking me for a favor. I don't remember what it was, but apparently I agreed to help her, and she seemed appreciative. She asked us jokingly, 'How old do you think I am?' My friend and I examined her: she was dressed in raggedy clothes and I don't think she was wearing any shoes, but despite that, she had an incredible presence. As if reading our thoughts, the woman said, 'I'm a great deal stronger than you think.'

"We didn't answer her, and left feeling a little strange. My friend and I decided we wanted to find a lookout point, and headed towards one we knew was nearby. As we made our way to the point, we suddenly heard the sound of hooves—a white horse came galloping past us seemingly out of nowhere with a young woman on its back. It went by very quickly and we soon lost sight of it. We continued on our way and a little further ahead, we saw a woman on the ground. Our first thought was that the woman had fallen off her horse and was injured. This woman was young and beautiful but looked strange, like she was part-serpent and part-human and had a divine presence about her. I can't remember what happened next, but after what seemed like only twenty minutes of time, I noticed two or three hours had passed. The woman had disappeared and I had no recollection of what had taken place in that missing time. Later, my friend and I guessed that the old woman, the horse, and the serpent woman on the trail were all the same being. Sure enough, there is an old Indian legend that shapeshifters and tricksters used to live in that area of Hidden Valley and Steep Rock.

"After these experiences I seemed to have some type of knowledge and knew that whoever this being was, she wanted me to bring my friends to Steep Rock to meet them. The being and others like her were looking for specific human blood types. I vaguely remember some type of initiation this woman performed wherein I was asked to drink a liquid or mist that enabled me see to things about their race. It turns out that the serpent woman is part of a very ancient race that once lived in the Hidden Valley area, but has since left. On occasion, I would go up to the hill with friends and we would meditate. The serpent people taught me how to communicate with them and leave our bodies. However, they told us that one person had to stay behind to make sure our bodies were safe.

"I had a great number of interdimensional experiences with these beings over the course of the next few months but only remember vague details. I learned that these beings were shapeshifters who lived in another dimension in the Steep Rock–Hidden Valley area a long time ago. In one communication experience, the serpent lady pointed to the position of the North Star, moved her arm to the left, and said, 'When we lived here, it was over there.' The serpent woman told me that her people's bodies were underground in a state of suspension and that most of them existed only spiritually. She said there was an underground mound and passage leading to a burial chamber in Hidden Valley that because of flooding was now accessible. She then asked me to bring buckets of water from the river to a particular location and leave them for another being to pick them up. She said I shouldn't stay to watch the entity that would appear to fetch the water because I would be frightened or confused by the way it looked, which might prove dangerous. I didn't really understand why the serpent woman wanted my help and what the buckets of water were for, but I obliged them nonetheless.

"After completing my chore, the serpent woman found me and told me that her people were attacked by an evil power a long time ago; many died because these serpent people didn't defend themselves—it was their way. She told me this happened because the age changed and their protective force field failed. She told me thirty thousand of them used to live in Steep Rock and Hidden Valley. I strongly felt this particular being (whom I later nicknamed the 'divine princess' for some reason) was a guardian of the area, protecting the rest of her race, who are sleeping. These shapeshifters came to our planet in ships from another world and became our ancient gods. An epic battle with a rival race took place, and the defeated serpent people fled to another dimension—ours—where they now dwell. She told me her people's stasis will end in eight hundred years. The 'divine princess' pointed to the sky, indicating the constellation we call the Pleiades and said that when conditions are right—a clear night with no frost or snow on the ground—they travel to that distant cluster of stars.

"The serpent people were able to reach out to me because of the things I experienced in the past. When I began hiking in the area, the 'divine princess' saw that I was able to communicate with them, so they initiated contact with me. I think they had been waiting to speak with someone for a while, but I was the first one they found compatible. I know it sounds crazy but everything I've told you is true. I can't remember all the experiences I've had in Steep Rock—what I've mentioned here is just the tip of the iceberg. I wish there was some way to remember everything, but most of it is unclear. I now live in New York City and try to return to Steep Rock to hike and bring friends to see what I experienced."

In the winter of 2009, I was going to meet Bruce at Steep Rock and visit the locations where he had his experiences, as the park and forest were not far from my home. Unfortunately, I never made it—my car wouldn't start. At first I thought the problem was a dead battery, but the next day, the engine turned over just fine. I brought the car, still relatively new, to the dealer to have it checked out. They couldn't find anything wrong with the vehicle—the battery was in excellent shape. Was my car trouble a coincidence, or did someone (or something) not want me at Steep Rock that day? I guess I'll never know for sure.

In the late winter of 2009, Rosemary Ellen Guiley and I paid a visit to Steep Rock and walked its trails for several hours. The landscape had a strange feel to it, as if by walking it, one would become lost in time. The winding trails had a mystical look that could have been used for filming the *Lord of the Rings* trilogy. I plan to meet Bruce in the near future and revisit this very unique place.

# NINE

# SAILING OFF THE EDGE OF REALITY

The contact experience takes place on many levels, including ones that happen but are not immediately recognized as such. A person can lead a normal existence, complete with all the good things life has to offer, and then one day without warning, he or she has contact with a nonhuman intelligence and is thrust into a new reality. I believe all close encounters are a form of contact, and at times, they may be so subtle that the individual may not recognize those strange events as such until years later.

I received the following letter from a physician who had multiple experiences in the past with ghost-like voices that could be considered a kind of dimensional contact. Although she has no conscious recollection of being abducted or meeting alien beings, she did see a UFO on November 15, 2008, in Nevada. I thought it was important to include the woman's letter because it serves as a good example of a credible

217

person who has been taken out of our mundane reality and plunged into the world of the paranormal.

### The Dark Triangle in the Sky

"It was about four in the morning and I was in my car, driving just outside Las Vegas with the sunroof open to get some desert air. Suddenly, I felt the car vibrating in an odd way. It was a bone-jarring vibration that was strangely noiseless. I looked around to see if something was wrong with my car, but nothing was out of the ordinary. Finally, I looked up at the dark sky and saw the star field disappear above me for a very wide distance in front and behind the road I was on. I took my foot off the gas and pulled into the slow lane. There in the sky was a triangular blackness that was *huge!* It was traveling very slowly, keeping perpendicular to the highway. I was pretty excited, and started waving and honking at passing truckers, pointing up to the sky. Thinking back, it was probably too dark and the other drivers must've thought I was nuts.

"The craft couldn't have been going more than forty miles per hour; it moved very slowly over my car and toward the mountains. There were no lights or markings on it anywhere and it was completely noiseless—the only reason I had seen it was because it blocked out the stars. I could see the lights from the strip even at this early morning hour, and as the object moved in that direction, it muddily reflected the strip's brilliant lights on its bottom until it had passed over. As it continued north, it vanished over the mountains. I know there's a military base in the direction I saw it leave.

"My engine wasn't affected and I didn't experience any missing time, but since my sighting, I've been hearing a strange voice. I don't know what it's saying or where it's from. It's all been in my head and could possibly be explained if an alien intelligence is communicating with me from another dimension."

What I like about the above report is that it once again shows that whoever or whatever is operating the triangular UFOs is very bold and couldn't care less how many people see it (see chapter two for more). The physician's account is also a good example of a close encounter and a very subtle form of contact.

## THE INTERDIMENSIONAL MANIPULATORS

The case below involves an individual named "Pete" who has an engineering background he believes has made him logical and practical. As the years passed, events would unfold in his life that would forever change the way he looked at the universe.

Pete contacted me in 2009 after hearing me on a radio show. He wanted to discuss his experiences, believing they related to my research. Pete says his experiences are dimensional in nature and are related to the UFO and alien contact phenomena. Originally a mechanical engineer who worked for the Department of Defense, Pete says his interest in UFOs and astronomy can be traced to his early childhood. He loved reading all kinds of books about astronomy and UFOs. Pete's fascination with the subject matter increased considerably as a teenager (in the seventies) but after that, he admits he lost interest because the material became very repetitive. It was only in the past three or four years that Pete's interest has been renewed; he has once again started reading all the new material out there. As a born-again UFO enthusiast, Pete has engaged in conversations with many others like him, and has found that half of them had also had experiences with UFOs and the paranormal. It was becoming clear to him that many people out there have had contact or other UFO-related experiences. He realized it was an influential part of our culture that sadly remains mostly hidden from the general public.

Pete felt a great deal of information flowing into him, and when he woke up one morning, something changed: for some reason, everything was clear to him and he could see things in a completely different way. Pete said that while walking in public, he could sense other people's life forces. He also began having incredible experiences in which things were much clearer and vibrant; he felt like some type of energy was inside him. His new awareness made him realize that an unseen universe surrounds us. He thought that perhaps when someone sees a UFO, they might be having a spiritual experience that wouldn't otherwise exist in our dimensional level. The spiritual concept opened him up to the idea that the contact phenomenon is not composed of nuts and bolts—there's a lot more to it.

As time went on, Pete felt that the information and situations coming to his attention were more than a coincidence. He felt directed to walk or drive in various directions, and when he followed, he would eventually meet a person who claimed to be in contact with extraterrestrials. After meeting many people this way, Pete's experiences began taking place at a level that was not physical, but part of what he calls the "spiritual realm." One of the people he met claimed to be in contact with an alien intelligence. This person called Pete one day and said there were probes and devices attached to Pete that connected with a ship. Information was being sent to this ship, piloted by an alien intelligence. The person told him these devices couldn't be seen; they existed just outside our reality, partially in another dimension. I found this last statement quite interesting because in the past years, several abductees or contact experiencers claim feeling connected with various alien intelligences, and that they were actually unwillingly sending the beings information about our human condition on Earth.

Pete discovered there are intelligences that influence us from different dimensional levels, planting subtle ideas in our minds. Pete believes the process is a slowly progressing manipulation of our identities and believes whoever is doing it has been doing so for a very long time. Because of this, Pete feels there is an interdimensional intelligence interfering with our growth. This intelligence's ultimate goal is to prevent the human race from attaining enlightenment.

Over the past two years, Pete claims to have been able to delve into these dimensional spaces and remove negative influences attached to himself and other people. As a (possible) result, disturbing things have taken place: people he knows or interact with have been showing classic signs of being abducted, including missing time, vivid dreams about aliens, and marks on the body. One morning Pete woke up and looked at the clock: it was 8:15 AM. He got up, went to his computer and the clock read 9:15 AM. Somewhere in between, Pete lost an hour of time. He now feels that the alien intelligence that is attracted to him is also taking an interest in the people he associates with.

Pete's contact with the intelligence in this other dimension is increasing and he says he's beginning to see a number of different species that exist in this other realm. He describes some as insectoid, others as looking like the classical gray aliens, and in rare cases, they look like lumbering trolls. In one of these otherworldly visions, Pete saw Native American shamans who had projected themselves into this dimension trying to stop some of the negative beings from attacking people in our world. Once again we see the Native American involvement in the contact situation, especially when the person was dealing with "negative" entities. Laura's story in chapter five of enlisting a shaman's aid is another example of this. The connection between Native American beliefs and the dimensional universe is quite strong and appears frequently in the contact experience.

Pete continues to have experiences with dimensional beings. On April 9, he wrote to me, describing his encounter.

"An elemental spirit visited my realm to connect with me this morning. It appeared as a rough, ten- to twelve-foot-tall, humanoid figure formed out of a material combined of wood and rock. It lumbered around and seemed to change shape as it walked. On the neck was a collar of jagged material resembling the fractured trunk of a hollow tree or perhaps a vertical outcrop of thinned rocks, like stalagmites forming a circle. Inside this area was a translucent sphere glowing with a mist surrounding it. A ball of light moved outwards from the center, like an energetic but unformed eye, vacillating slowly as we communicated. Much of what it presented seemed only to be a confirmation of messages we are getting from all around us today. It provided details that put certain concepts into a greater perspective, perhaps the crux of the effort.

"The elemental being came to me to discuss the true nature of the planets, moons, stars, and other celestial bodies in our universe. Apparently, they are no different in function and relation to each other than the cells in our bodies—part of our composite physical being and individually alive and purposeful, but all the while connected to a larger, more complex physiology. This mega-construct ultimately and collectively creates the physical and spiritual structure of our universe. All the planets, moons, stars and galaxies are a vast material expression of the raw, immutable source energy making up all of creation. There is within them a form of spiritual essence that is unique and vastly different in form and scale from anything we can easily conceive. This is a truth that has been lost to us. Individually, each planet radiates an energy signature or celestial life frequency that represents the harmony of all its physical and nonphysical or dimensional components combined. In our case, the Earth's mass, rocks molten and solid, water, soil, atmosphere, magnetism, gravity, organic elements, living creatures, plants, and animals combine with that enormous spiritual essence into something of which we are an integrated part. Each planetary body is, of course, unique. For example, the radiant and strong energetic vibrancy of the Earth is in contrast to the cool, mellow signature of our moon, but both are obviously connected and interdependent, each influencing the personality and celestial identity of the other. The relationship of the Earth and moon is no coincidence. Unfortunately, it is quite evident that man has become disconnected from the primordial Earth frequency; we no longer live in sync with the pulse of our home world. Through a number of mechanisms and forces, cultural and social as well as evolutionary, we have arrived at a point where our presence is damaging the very planet that bore us into existence and sustains us still. No longer living in close relationship to nature, we have lost that critical link back to the Earth source. In fact, the analogy I was given is that now we are acting as invading ants in the hair of our own life-giving planet, irritating and disrupting the symbiotic relationship that must exist between any living being and its life source.

"Sadly, we've heard much of this message before. It's played out to us repeatedly in different ways, every day through all media. Despite the warnings, we continue on a path divergent from the essential unity that must exist for the well-being of humanity and our planet. Many ancient and indigenous cultures acknowledged and embraced this relationship, though not always to our modern understanding (or approval). We've had the answers in the past—there's no reason we can't learn them again. The message was to reconnect mankind, lest we kill the life-giving mother of us all.

"Other information that came through was of a more unusual nature. It was suggested that a select few extraterrestrial beings (physical and nonphysical/dimensional) are attempting to influence or intervene in human affairs to redirect us off our destructive path. The elemental was implying that these extraterrestrials are on Earth, essentially working as antibodies in the interest of the larger universe, attempting to contain a vile malignancy that is harming a unique planetary entity. The good of the whole universe is their primary goal, reuniting humanity and Earth."

## Contact Through Dreams

In some cases, contact is made in an unconscious or semiconscious state, as if to gently condition or prepare the person. As time goes on, the individual may develop psychic abilities, the majority of which develop exceptional skills as painters or illustrators. The gifted individual might paint images they've seen in their dreams showing unearthly landscapes and nonhuman entities. In most of these so-called "dreams," the person is slowly given information over an extended period of time and shown pictures, symbols, and sometimes even video projections of events that will transpire in Earth's future. Before you discount a contact encounter that takes place in the dream state, please remember that there are many cultures and religions who firmly believe that the divine, angels, or other beings communicate with selected individuals while they sleep. The examples in history are much too numerous to cover in this chapter, but one can use the resources in this book's bibliography to obtain more information on the subject. The next case involves a middle-aged woman who had encounters with alien-like creatures as a child and then vivid dreams as an adult about these same aliens and their purpose. I consider what she's experienced more than just dreams—they are a telepathic form of contact. Although I do not have room in this book to include all the dreams of contact she's had, the most important were selected. This individual would like to be known simply as "Silver" (not to be confused with Rosemary Ellen Guiley's "Silver Lady" from the previous chapter). If any of my readers would like to contact her, please write to me at the address in the appendix.

### When Dreams Are a Part of Reality

The first experience took place when Silver was five years old, living in Florida. She woke up one night confused, looked out the window, and saw four or five odd-looking dog-like creatures walking across the yard heading toward the forest area near her house. As Silver watched, the creatures stopped, turned in unison, and stared at her. This really spooked her so she let go of the curtain and ran away from the window. She doesn't remember the time, but knew it was late because everybody else in the house was asleep. When Silver turned around to flee, she saw someone standing in the middle of the room. This person was about five feet tall, slender, and wearing a cape with a tall, vampire-like collar that hid part of "her" face. Not seeing the mouth move, possibly using mental telepathy, the person told Silver, "You are not supposed to be up. You have to go to bed." Normally not a rude child and for some reason rather bold, Silver replied, "You're not my mama and you can't tell me what to do!" After that sighting, she continued to have sightings of unusual lights and strange dreams, most of which she can remember clearly.

Silver had many more experiences, one of which took place in 1994: She woke up and saw two gray beings alongside her while lying in bed. Each being took one of her arms and "floated" her through the closed window of her bedroom. As they passed through the glass, she describes the feeling of her molecular self moving like "passing through jell-o." Once outside the house, she and the beings were taken upward by a light into a small craft. Silver was then led into a room where she saw gadgets and all types of technical control panels, some being manned by Grays or other beings. In this room, she saw people who acted like zombies. They were sitting behind a long table with dividers between them. It looked like some of the beings were a cross between the Grays and humans, but they were cooperating with them. Silver recognized one of the people as her uncle. She felt the gray beings wanted her to see everything happening. She remembers seeing one person who looked more human than Gray sitting by a table doing something (she can't remember exactly what).

Silver also remembers seeing a number of other different types of beings; one type she calls the "troll people" she didn't like because they came out of her closet at night. Silver thought they looked scary: they wore hoods over their heads and were short and stocky. After the ship visitation,

Silver woke up in her bed, wondering if what she had seen was a dream or a real experience. As for the troll people, Silver is more willing to talk about them as an adult. One particular encounter is still fresh in her mind as she relates it below.

"I was eleven years old and it was 1963. I was terrified to be in my bedroom at night with the lights out. I always covered my head with a blanket and would lie very still. On this night, after I was able to feel more relaxed, I slowly removed the lightweight cover from eyes and looked into the closet. There, I saw an ugly face staring at me from the darkness. I didn't wait to find out what it was, so I whipped the covers back over my head. I could feel my heart beating in my throat, almost choking me and making the whole bed seem to shake. Somehow I fell asleep and had an awful 'dream' where I saw what looked like a very short, blunt-faced troll creature. Its wrinkled, wide-eyed face poked out of a hood the same brown color as its outer coverings. The creature may have been three feet tall, I'm not sure; all I know is that it was short, bulky, and ugly. I knew it was there to take me away. It walked up to me, seized my ankle with a strong grip, and pulled me toward the closet. In the closet was a shiny, gray light in the middle of which was a hole. The troll was trying to pull me towards the hole. I clawed and grabbed for anything I could find to try and keep this thing from taking me away. I don't know how the whole thing ended; the next thing I knew, I was in bed and it was a bright sunny day."

It's interesting to note that in many of the cases I've investigated, the entities come from a hole in a dark or dimly lit closet to enter the room. In at least one case in my files, the person saw a green or bluish light in the closet and walked over to investigate. When the man, then twenty-five years old, entered the large walk-in closet, a black hole materialized in the center and two glowing, yellow hands came and grabbed his arms. The hands then tried to pull this person into the hole, but he was able to break free. In one mighty burst of energy, the man fell backwards, breaking the phantom hands' hold. The "hole" closed up and the closet was once again dark. Do beings that live in a parallel dimension periodically open portals to take people, or are these types of occurrences nothing more than dreams?

Silver's contact experiences continued through most of her adult life and, like Laura in chapter five, she has noticed paranormal activity seems to run in the family. She knows for sure that her children have had nighttime encounters with the Grays on more than one occasion. However, unlike Silver, they are afraid of the beings and don't want anything to do with them. Silver's son, who is now twenty-seven years old, once woke up in the middle of the night and saw a Gray standing by his bed. He was very scared and took a swing at it but only hit air—the being vanished. Her daughter also reported that on many occasions she would wake up to see a blue light in the room and hear whispering voices.

On December 17, 1993, Silver would have the following contact experience. Luckily, she was keeping a journal after each "dream" so the information is well documented.

"I was by a roaring river, other people were around. A huge spaceship appeared overhead and beamed us aboard.

We didn't want to go, but had no choice. Once aboard, we met people who handed us clothes to put on. They looked human, but we knew they had taken human-like forms so we wouldn't be afraid of them. With me on the ship were two guys and three women; we were all put in the same room together. I was amazed at the expanse of this craft; the aliens had created a realistic, Earth-like surface inside. I told the other people with me that the aliens wanted to impregnate the women because they were trying to cross-breed with us to make themselves better. We left the room and found an empty one made of shiny material. In that room, we saw a chute but couldn't tell what it is used for. We guessed there was a room at the end of the chute and wondered if it was a means of escape. So, we went down the chute to another room that had a window. At first, no one was there, so we carefully walked towards the window. Suddenly, other human-type aliens surrounded us, but they didn't seem to be paying us any attention. The 'people' seem to be drugged or fixed in some way that made them robotic. We went to the window and were able to escape. Once we were out of the craft, I wondered if we were really outside or if the aliens just let us think we were. We ran across some rough terrain and suddenly heard a vehicle approaching. We scrambled to the side of the road and hid in some bushes. The vehicle went by, and I knew it was the aliens looking for us. As we made our escape, we finally saw a fence and on the other side, a farmhouse and a barn. There were a couple of cars and a truck parked in the yard. A woman in a calf-length dress came right up to the fence. She was friendly and we knew she wouldn't hand us over to the aliens. She motioned for us to follow her to the house, inside, to a back room with a hallway. Somehow, I was spotted by the aliens, who were crudely disguised as a sheriff, deputy, and a couple of men. I climbed into the attic to hide and they came after me. I managed to escape."

A number of my writings mention the UFO experience as incredibly complex and possibly involving beings from several different origins. One type of these beings may be the djinn (introduced in chapter six). Another type of being associated with the contact experience are what UFO investigators call the "Nordics." The Nordics are tall, with very long blonde or red hair, blue or green eyes, and light skin. They seem to be more angelic in nature and have often protected humans against negative entities. In some cases, the Nordics teach the people they contact and give them philosophical or technical information. Below is a contact "dream" experience from May 31, 1995, in which Silver and her husband encountered both types of beings.

### The Shapeshifter and the Angel

In this contact experience, Silver was with her husband walking on a rural road when suddenly, a man appeared about thirty feet away. Silver describes him as about 5'5" with dark hair and a broad, husky build. She got the sense that the man didn't like them and could cause them harm. Suddenly, he changed into a lizard-like creature that stood upright like a man. As the creature started walking towards them, he said something to her husband that immobilized him. Her husband fell to the ground. The shapeshifter continued to walk towards them, but before it could reach them, Silver picked her husband up as he was trying to come out of his daze. Just then, a huge, broad-shouldered giant appeared: a seven- to eight-foot-tall man with blonde, shoulder-length hair. The "giant" wore robe-type garments that appeared to be multicolored, patterned, or layered in some other way. Silver doesn't remember what the giant's face looked like, but she knew the being was there to help them. He came up to them, touched her husband on his back and Silver on her head and arm, and she blacked out. She knew this being had power over the lizard creature and would not let it harm them. Silver wrote later that she felt the beings could be among us, and because they are able to alter their shapes, we would never know it.

I have met many people who say they have dreamt of being abducted or contacted by aliens in their dreams. Are people actually taken out of their bodies by some unknown intelligence? If this is the case, the body would have to be separated from the spirit or soul somehow. The soul would experience the abduction or contact, and the body and brain would be left behind and continue to dream. When the soul is placed back into the body and mind, body and soul once again merge. The contact experience itself may combine the brain's dreams, causing the person to remember mixed or confusing images. As incredible as this theory may sound, we may have to broaden our ideas of how alien intelligence may contact us. I have many case files in which an abduction or contact took place in the so-called astral state.

# TEN

# ALIEN SYMBOLS
# AND LANGUAGE

The majority of religions and cultural mythologies often provide their own explanations for the origin and development of the written language. Most mythologies do not credit humans with the invention of language; in the legends it is often stolen, or given to humans by a supernatural being. Depending on the time period and the culture, these beings can be gods, spirits of nature, or even angels or the djinn. In Egypt, the god Thoth is said to have given to the Egyptians the gift or writing. A similar story exists in other ancient cultures, such as in pre-Columbian Mexico, where Quetzalcoatl gave the gift of writing to the Aztec people. In most cases, these gods appeared out of nowhere or descended from the sky to instruct humans and help them establish a stable civilization. No matter how many books you read on the subject, no one knows for sure how the written word came about. The earliest known script, dating back to 3500 BCE, is said to be Sumerian cuneiform, written in the ancient language of the Sumer people of Mesopotamia. Legends and various religious texts mention a time when all the people of the world had one written and spoken language. God, or some other supernatural being, decided this was not good for the human race and intervened.

One of the best-known examples is the story of the Tower of Babel from the biblical book of Genesis. The passage, common to Judaism and Christianity (but not to Islam), tells of God punishing man for the tower's construction by means of creating so many different languages that the people working on it couldn't communicate with each other. Local variations of this passage were used by Christian missionaries in the sixteenth century to encourage people of the "new world" to speak English, French, or Spanish. A group of people on the island of Polynesia tell a very similar story to the Tower of Babel, speaking of a god who "in anger chased the builders away, destroyed the building with lightning, and changed the language of the people so that they spoke diverse tongues."[1] In Islam, the differences in human language are considered the will of Allah: "And of his signs are the creation of the heavens and the earth and the diversity of your tongues [languages]."[2] However, if you look at this passage closely, it indicates that once again, a supernatural being was responsible for giving humanity language.

Besides the many different types of script that have appeared on this planet in the last five thousand years, a num-

---

1 Williamson, R.W. *Religious and Cosmic Beliefs of Central Polynesia.* Cambridge, UK: Cambridge Press, 1933.

2 (Qur'an 30:22)

ber of unknown forms have emerged that can't be traced to any one group of people. In the days of the European Renaissance, this language was considered magical in nature, believed to be used in communication with otherworldly beings such as elves, fairies, leprechauns, and the host of angels. Today, these mysterious symbols and scripts continue to show up as a written form of "alien" language.

## The Roswell Hieroglyphs

One of the most famous forms of "alien script" in UFO lore comes from the alleged Roswell UFO crash in 1947. For those of you not familiar with this case, a brief synopsis of the incident is presented here.

During a violent thunderstorm on the night of July 4, residents of southern New Mexico reported seeing an exceptionally bright flash of light in the sky followed by a loud explosion. The next day, Mac Brazel, a rancher near the city of Corona, discovered metallic debris on his property, some of which he stuffed into a sack. On July 6, Brazel drove to Roswell and brought the fragments to a Sheriff Wilcox. Sheriff Wilcox was so intrigued by the material that he called the local army base. When intelligence officer Jesse Marcel came out to examine the pieces, he was similarly mystified, and decided to accompany Brazel back to the ranch. On July 7, Marcel toured the ranch, collecting more bits of debris, which he took home and showed to his wife and son. Although the substance was easily crumpled like tin foil, it would promptly return to its original shape. With the debris was a beam of metal featuring unknown symbols that looked like hieroglyphs.

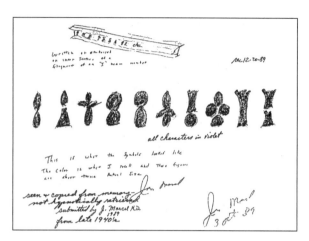

*Roswell UFO glyphs*
*(Photo credit: author)*

*Roswell paper headlines covering alien crash incident*
*(Photo credit: public domain)*

Much later, Marcel's adult son drew the symbols to the best of his recollection. The air force would later claim that what Brazel and Marcel found on the ranch was nothing more than scraps from a weather balloon. It was also explained that the so-called symbols were designs on a strip of plastic tape used to hold components of the balloon together. To this day, the "hieroglyphs" from the material found on the ranch at Corona have never been positively identified as being alien, or as the markings used by any commercial tape company.

Over the years, I have collected pages of "alien writings" and symbols from people who claim contact in one form or another. The problem is that much of the script looks like nothing more than incoherent scribbles to me, but in some cases "alien symbols" would come to my attention that looked like the real thing. These cases will be presented in this chapter with as much background information as possible.

## The Angelic Script of Dean Fagerstrom

Dean Fagerstrom's amazing contact case with a being called Donestra appears in chapter three. In addition to the other amazing things Mr. Fagerstrom was able to produce, he also wrote eight pages of unknown symbols Donestra channeled through him. The channeling took place in the summer of 1981 when Dean was on night duty as a security guard at a shopping center in Mount Kisco, New York. His job was routine—nothing of significance ever took place, but on this night, he felt as if there was a presence in that dark building with him. After his hourly rounds, he sat at his desk and closed his eyes for what seemed like a minute. When he opened them, he realized that an hour or so had passed. In front of him, written on the back of company time sheets were lines of unknown symbols. Dean gave me these sheets in 1982, and since that time, I've worked on deciphering their meaning. I showed the symbols to a number of cryptographers and linguistics experts, but despite their combined experience, no one was able to give me any answers. I was told that the symbols seem to be a real language (not scribble), and that there are at least two hundred unique characters in the pages I have. A little over twenty-five years later, I finally was able to decipher some of Dean's channeled messages. The script Dean produced is made up of symbols and letters from over fifty different languages, of which thirty no longer exist. In the script are Greek, angelic script, Gregg shorthand, cuneiform, Hebrew, Sanskrit, Arabic, and several other languages I haven't been able to identify. In Dean's alien script, each character is combined with several letters from one known and one unknown alphabet, making it appear unfamiliar and strange. If Dean faked the channeling, the fact that he was able to write this is amazing in itself. Dean has no idea what the script means but feels strongly it is angelic in nature. The script below is a scanned copy of the original and represents one of eight pages.

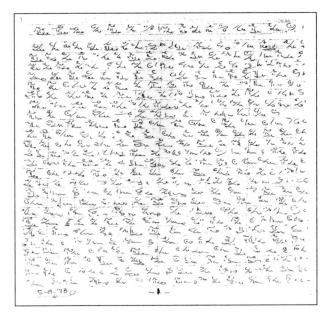

*Donestra alien script*
*(Photo credit: author)*

### Translation

Dean (or Donestra) also supplied one page that had not only the alien script, but also English words and letters below it. Although there was not enough information to translate every page, I was slowly able to translate some of what Donestra channeled through Dean Fagerstrom with a great deal of work and time. Most of the pages are about technologies and realms of existence higher than the physical plane. The translation for the preceding script is below; accuracy of the translation is as close as possible under the circumstances.

Out of Orion's Mouth come seven declarations of things that are done and things to come. The first of these is the great dark hollow within the Earth which shall bring forth destruction from the beast lying within. Out of Orion's mouth proceeds the destruction of the ages, and from his eye, on top of his pillar, a light shall be seen. To those who are called the children of Light, there shall be a new vision of both hope and joy, but those who are not called the children of Light shall find destruction, and be cast into the darkness. Look to the high places—even the mountains—and seek the lonely places . . . these are the safe places from the great destroyer called Sadden.

It's obvious that this first part of the script translation is referring to the constellation of Orion. Orion was known as the Hunter, the Giant, and in Egypt, the constellation was associated with the god Osiris. In the Torah, the constellation is identified with the Nephilim, a race of giants who were created out of the union of humans and angels. There is a reference in here similar to the information given in other contact/channeling experiences of a devastating cosmic event that will emerge and bring catastrophe to humans on Earth.

The second part of the translation is much different; it almost seems as if another author replaced Dean to channel its information. This second voice speaks of another universe parallel to our own—a place it calls the one "true" reality—of which our physical universe is merely a projection. A very rough translation is given below.

There are six realms in nature called "matter." There are three prior to these, called "highest modes." Energy is manifested in all nature through a sequential emission of the six lower modes in a successive manner. The origin of energy is contained within the three highest modes; these modes proceed in succession from the highest to the innermost source and should rightly be called the very life of the physical universe. The hexagon is the shape for all six modes. Through its shape, all external mechanics needed for the successive tuning, universal resonance, and corresponding energy levels are derived, therefore appearing in countless manifestations within the most external domain in nature. There is a connection between the three highest modes and the six lower modes, seen as a large disc with countless openings in the hexagonal shape of the universe. This is called the neutral disc and is the creation point of a sixth particle that controls the lower modes. To invoke the great energetic manifestation within the domain of the physical universe, it is necessary to tune in the six lower modes together. This results in one succession of overtones which resonates in degrees toward the highest mode. Energy is then sent from the highest to the lowest mode. This is in accord with successive and simultaneous manifestations that are active or passive. Each mode within the six lower modes expresses a greater formation in its matrix of construction. This must be seen as a three-dimensional object, such as a cone or spiral. The cone can be reversed, thus producing an inverted manifestation. All minerals, animals, and planets in the physical universe are created through energy resonated through the six lower modes in a matrix-like fashion. In the formation of the human mind is a neutral energy built into the matrix which acts like a veil between the three highest modes and six lower modes. It is possible that the human mind can align this neutral energy, polarize it so its rotation will permeate a higher energy, and rise above the lower six modes. It can also take in other living things in the physical universe, but the process is more mechanistic.

After this portion, the author seems to change yet again, but I haven't been able to translate the rest. It seems that as the author changes, the symbols are used in slightly different ways, changing their meaning. Also, I'd like to note that this form of script is very compact; the one page presented earlier translates into at least twenty-three pages in English.

## Alien Alphabet

In chapter nine, I introduced Silver and her "dream" contact experiences. As a result or byproduct of her numerous contact experiences, she was able to list some of the alien symbols with their English representations, appearing below. During one of these experiences, a "gray" alien being raised Silver's arm, wanting her to look at it. When she did, Silver noticed symbols on her arm. Later, when Silver regained consciousness, she drew what she could remember. Although some of the symbols Silver envisioned are almost identical to what others have written, it's impossible at this time to make any sense as to what they mean. I could find some of the symbols from my previous work and substituted English letters for them, but I must be missing the cipher because no matter how the letters are arranged, they make no sense. I discovered later that Silver's script contains letters from the following ancient languages: Ogham, Aramaic, Iberian, and Greek. The symbols painted on her arm contain the letters G, D, H, M, V, and Q. This is the only part I can translate; some of the other symbols are indecipherable at this point in my research. I could only find letters for the left side of her paintings that feature the script; they include the following: M, D, H, V, G, and F.

## Other Forms of "Alien Writings"

The following two examples of alien symbols also contain representations of characters from several earthly languages. I have not been able to decipher them as yet; perhaps we'll never know what they mean. The first is from a person who claims to have had several abduction experiences, while the second example is from an individual who channels "Omada," an angelic-like being. Neither individual has any idea what the symbols mean. What was presented in this chapter represents only a small sample of unknown symbols I have collected over the years from contactees, abductees, and people who claim to channel aliens, spirits, angels, and other beings.

*Alien writing example 1*
*(Photo credit: author)*

*Alien writing example 2*
*(Photo credit: author)*

# ELEVEN

# IS THERE A
# GOVERNMENT COVER-UP?

Since the 1950s, people with great interest in the UFO phenomenon have thought the US government knows more
than it is willing to admit, concealing and suppressing the
spread of information. Some enthusiasts also claim the military and a "special unit" within the FBI have been keeping tabs on people who have claimed contact. This train of
thought has persisted into the twenty-first century; today, a
good number of paranormal investigators are obsessed with
believing conspiracy theories revolving around UFOs.

I've been a speaker at many UFO conferences where it
was not uncommon to hear attendees who were very gung-
ho about the conspiracy theories accuse certain UFO investigators of being government spies or plants. In the late
eighties and well into the nineties, several UFO researchers
started rumors that I was working for the government, spying on people who were involved in investigations and attending conferences just to mine information I would later

relay to the CIA. I believe this all started when one particularly paranoid UFO investigator saw my name in a military document dated 1974 mentioning CIA operations in southeast Asia. Well, for the record, I've never concealed the fact from anyone that in my military service (from 1969 to 1974), I was assigned to a unit that was involved in medical operations during the Vietnam war. At the time, however, I had no idea who was running the show and always did only what I was told. The two operations I was involved in concerned combat support operations—nothing to do with UFOs. Unfortunately, for many years, the lunatic contingent in UFO circles believed I was reporting to a "secret" agency. To set the record straight, I am *not* working for the government and have had no official connection with the military since my honorable discharge in 1974.

Sadly, quite a few researchers in the field are bent on believing that the government is trying to disrupt their investigations and silence them. Well, the government doesn't need to expend any resources to silence anyone; with all the finger-pointing and arguing within the UFO community, they're proving to be their own worst enemy! But the question remains: is there really a government cover-up? The US government is huge; I find it hard to believe that everyone in Congress or the military is the keeper of all the secrets. I believe that a small part of the government attached to our intelligence agencies does in fact have information about UFOs, hidden from the public, Congress, and the military. Reasons for the concealment can vary: it might be because the truth is so shocking that many Americans may not be able to handle it, or at the very least, they believe the time isn't right. It's certainly true that the smaller the number of people who know a secret, the better the chance there is of it not being discovered. I've had numerous contacts with members of various intelligence organizations and the military during my investigations and except for the New York Power Authority (after the Indian Point nuclear reactor sightings), no agency has ever tried to prevent me from researching UFOs.

## Mystery Aircraft at Stewart

During the first week of November in 1983, several months after the grand appearance of the Hudson River Valley UFO, witnesses reported seeing mysterious lights in the night sky. This time, the lights turned out to be nothing more than a number of planes flying in a very tight "military" formation. There was no doubt that these lights were in fact conventional aircraft; many highly trained people stood right under them as they passed over their heads. Many of these same people had also seen the giant UFO on an earlier date and were unable to identify it, yet they were able to identify what they saw as planes in formation. As the lights passed over, most could definitely hear engine noise from multiple aircraft, and the lights did not keep a consistent distance in relation to each other. The pilots were good, but it was difficult to keep the aircraft steady enough to appear as one object.

The mystery planes were also observed by several witnesses using binoculars. These witnesses were able to draw the shapes of the aircraft they had seen. The drawings were all very similar, so I sent them to a couple of pilots I knew in order to identify the aircraft. One pilot is an ex-military pilot, the other is an ex-commercial airline pilot who also used to fly missions for the CIA. Both pilot consultants agreed that the aircraft drawings were of the Cessna O-2.

The O-2 is a medium-duty aircraft with a single or double engine, capable of long-range flights. The CIA and other intelligence agencies use this type of aircraft frequently. Typically, the O-2 is used for surveillance missions and has very quiet, muffled engines. The newer models even have onboard flight computers that enable low-risk formation flying. I have reports that as many as eight planes have been seen flying together in tight formation. Whoever the pilots were, they were very talented, since on the several nights they were seen, the winds gusted to over twenty-five miles an hour yet the pilots were still able to keep formation.

In response to the many reports of what was now apparently small aircraft attempting to fake a UFO, I put together a team and staked out a number of strategic locations over the next several weeks. On more than one occasion we were able to see the planes and track them from the ground. There was no doubt about it—these pilots were very good and the aircraft they flew produced very little engine noise. It was apparent that the pilots were trying to fake a UFO, possibly attempting to discredit the real sightings that had recently taken place. It's important to note that most of the plane sightings occurred on Thursday nights, the official night for air force night maneuvers. From 1983 to the present day, these mystery aircraft have also been reported throughout the northeastern United States, shortly after major UFO sightings. My team had nine cars in the field, all equipped with amateur radio transceivers in addition to a home base with a radio kept in contact with the cars. We also monitored the police and aircraft bands for that area of New York. Dozens of residents in Putnam and Dutchess Counties had our base of operation's phone number and were asked to call if they saw any strange lights in the sky. Any information could then be relayed by radio to all the teams in the cars. If the mystery fliers were going to make an appearance, we'd have no trouble tracking them from the ground and hopefully we'd be able to discover their secret place of origin.

The planes would always fly for about two hours under a veil of darkness and then land, but where? They had been seen in the past circling Stormville Airport, located in Dutchess County. The planes gave the impression that they were going to land at this tiny airfield, but they didn't—they would break formation over the airport and head west. Only on one occasion did I receive a report of a single plane that broke from the group and landed at Stormville Airport, but no pilot ever got out. The plane stayed silent on the ground for several minutes and then took off, heading northwest. The witness noted that as the plane flew into the night sky, it never turned on its navigation lights. She also reported that the plane had no markings and was black in color.

After spending several nights on the roads with nothing to show for our time and effort, the planes finally appeared again on January 10, 1984, at 10 PM over the Hudson Valley skies, heading east. We first spotted them near I-84 near Carmel, and after making a number of maneuvers in the sky,

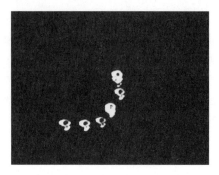

*The mystery planes seen over the Hudson Valley*
*trying to fake a UFO sighting*
*(Photo credit: author)*

they turned west. All teams in cars were alerted and for the next hour or so, we followed them from the ground. There were enough cars on the road so at least three to four teams always had them in sight, radioing the planes' position to the other cars. During the chase, I drove to a high ridge and watched them in binoculars as they passed almost directly overhead. I counted eight separate planes and could only see their outlines—the lights they were fitted with were definitely unconventional and lined up under the wings. The planes appeared to be painted a flat black; no part of any of the aircraft was illuminated. I was very surprised that eight aircraft flying at about 1,500 feet could make so little noise and estimated that each plane was no more than thirty feet from another in an amazing V formation. The lights would change from all white to green, red, and yellow; there seemed to be no lights on the nose or the tail. I thought to myself, "Whoever these pilots are, they must be violating FAA regulations!" We finally tracked the planes to Stewart

International Airport. Stewart is the site of an old Air Force Strategic Air Command (SAC) base that in 1970 was turned over to the New York Air National Guard and the Marine Corps. We parked our cars at a safe distance outside the security area and watched the planes land one at a time on the old SAC landing field, isolated from the main part of the airport. According to our research, this section of the base was supposed to have been closed down for the last twenty years. Although it was difficult to tell from our position, we thought the planes were taken into a large hangar or perhaps even underground. SAC bases were known for underground bays where aircraft could be hidden from aerial view and protected while not in use.

Several days later, during daylight hours, several team members and I visited Stewart Airport and found a large, isolated, fenced-off airfield far away from the main strip and terminal. The area was completely closed off, and there were many signs indicating that this was a secure area and that access was restricted. On the grounds were several buildings that looked like hangars. These buildings were large enough to house at least a dozen medium-sized planes. Although we were there for several hours, we didn't see any activity at all.

After our somewhat uneventful investigation, I filed a Freedom of Information Act (FOIA) request with the CIA to find out if they were using the area for some type of operation involving small aircraft. After several weeks, I received a lengthy letter explaining that the CIA had denied my request for information. Their reason was that they believed if they acknowledged their presence at Stewart, it would pose a threat to national security. The letter stated: "The Central Intelligence Agency can neither confirm nor deny its activities at Stewart Airfield. Any release of information about such alleged activities may in fact jeopardize the security of operatives and reveal the location of agents who provide information on matters of national security. Therefore, your request is denied for reasons that the information may be detrimental to the security of the United States and this office."

I strongly felt this letter was an admission that the CIA was operating out of the "closed down" area at Stewart and that the planes *did* belong to them. It is also apparent the pilots who were in control of these planes were experts with years of experience in close-formation flying. What was going on in this restricted area?

A short time after receiving my rejection letter, a member of the local Newburgh media contacted me, telling me about his experience while researching a news story at Stewart. This person said he found the restricted area on the base and was very curious as to what was going on there, as he had heard strange rumors for years. He climbed over the security fence, and out of nowhere, a jeep came screeching to a halt and three military police (air force) got out of the jeep and took him by force to a building just inside the gate. Once there, he was pushed into a chair, and told to sit still and remain quiet. The room was very dimly lit, and aside from several chairs and a table in the room, he didn't see any furnishings. After about fifteen minutes, two men entered the room dressed in dark suits. They began to question him. He tried to explain that he was doing a news story on Stewart based on stories from local residents and airport workers who told of covert military operations carried out in a part of the airport that was supposed to be shut down. One of the men had a computer printout in his hand, which had the journalist's name on it. He told me, "It was scary . . . they had this computer sheet with all this information—they knew everything about me." After about twenty minutes or so of being interrogated, one of them made a phone call. The journalist was then taken outside, placed in a car, and driven to the public area of the airport, where another agent had his car. He was then told by one of the men not to say anything about what had taken place. The agent told him, "If you know what's good for you, you'll forget about this entire incident." The journalist remains fearful to this day that the men who questioned him are still keeping an eye on him. He guesses they were CIA or another branch of military intelligence.

In my investigation of this restricted area, I discovered that the base now harbors several large C-5 Galaxy transport jets. On more than one occasion, I was able to photograph these military aircraft on the field. This type of aircraft is the largest cargo jet used by the United States Air Force. I actually witnessed a number of these cargo jets landing on the restricted airfield during the night; apparently they've been doing so for several years. The military still actively claims the airfield is closed, but if so, why is the flight line kept in immaculate condition, and why were these super transports—each the size of a 747—landing in the restricted area? I found out through a document search that the New York Air National Guard is no longer officially running the unrestricted area at Stewart. Since the early seventies, the base has been under naval and marine command. In my early days of UFO research, I would often come across documents that tied naval intelligence to the UFO phenomenon. Was the navy now here in the Hudson Valley trying to control the UFO situation? Could the mystery planes be piloted by naval aviators?

### USDA Involvement

I conducted extensive research, trying to find answers to the many questions I had about Stewart Airfield, and was able to find several documents indicating that the United States Department of Agriculture (USDA) was also using a section of the restricted area as a holding place for animals. The information in the documents indicated that a considerable number of cattle were being shipped to this location between 1984 and 1986. I considered this very strange, and wanted more information, so I placed a call with the USDA in Washington, DC. To my amazement, they gave me the number of their Stewart location. An operator connected me to the extension of a Ms. Amy Hunbert, public relations agent for USDA inquiries. When I asked about obtaining more information about the cattle shipments, she said that there had been so many cattle shipments to the Stewart receiving station over the last three years, I would have to be more specific in my request. I asked for all the documents of cattle shipments to Stewart from 1982 to 1989 and was told that she would have to clear it with her supervisor. She instructed me to call back the next day between two and four in the afternoon. I waited as she requested, and called. Ms. Hunbert told me that my request was quite large, and would have to be filed through the proper channels using the Freedom of Information Act. In the weeks to follow, I filed several Freedom of Information Act requests with the USDA, but after several months, I received no answer. I contacted the USDA once again at Stewart and was told that my request didn't arrive in time—all documents of the nature I had requested had been destroyed or erased from the main computer. The reason that they gave me was that after a certain number of years, they delete a great number of records "to save space." I found this answer unacceptable, but later an inside informer at the base confirmed that the documents involving the cattle shipments to Stewart Air Base had been destroyed because they held a dark secret of some kind of animal experimentation they wanted to keep from the public. Is it possible my inquiries were delayed on purpose so any tracks of what was going on could be erased?

What was the connection between the cattle being shipped into Stewart, the mystery planes, and the UFOs that had been seen in the Hudson Valley for many years? Some researchers have been making a connection between bizarre cattle mutilations in the southwest and the UFO phenomenon. Some believe an alien intelligence needs certain parts of the cattle to survive. Perhaps our government was trading large numbers of cattle for something they wanted from the aliens. Perhaps they were using Stewart as a holding and distribution point. I didn't know for sure, but the small aircraft that were trying to fake the UFO were definitely military and from Stewart.

My hypotheses would be confirmed in 1992 when I received a phone call from an individual who claimed to be a pilot of one of the planes. Although the caller didn't want to be taped, a brief account of his phone conversation with me is presented below. As he spoke, I wrote down what he was saying, word for word. The caller is a retired captain for American Airlines and also worked as a CIA operative. As an operative, his job was to pilot aircraft for the CIA and naval intelligence for missions he was always given limited information about. For example, on one of his "jobs" for the CIA, he was instructed to take one of their small aircraft to Cape Cod, pick up a passenger with a red briefcase, and bring him back to Stewart. He was never told who the person was and what was in the case. When he was told to fly in formation with the other pilots, he was given very little information about the mission.

## AN UNEXPECTED CALL

"I was one of the pilots who flew in formation over the Hudson Valley. Although I am retired now, I don't want my name used—I might be violating some national security clause. I was called by the chief of operations for the CIA in the northeast to carry out a number of night formation flying missions out of the old SAC field at Stewart Air Base. There were five other pilots including myself, all of us with more or less the same background. We were told to fly in formation around the Hudson Valley at an altitude of five thousand feet at about a 150 knots, very slow for formation flying. The aircraft we were using was the O-2A, which has a flight computer and a muffled engine. This aircraft is capable of long range and has great stability. We were told our flights were just test flights to check the computer's effectiveness during very close formation flying in windy conditions. I questioned the mission, however, because the planes were equipped with unconventional lighting and we were flying over a heavily populated area. I never received any explanations.

"We would fly over most of southern New York and some of Connecticut, then head north up to Cape Cod. From there, we swung around to the south and headed back to Stewart for a debriefing. I questioned these flights—it seemed like we were putting on a show for the people below. We were instructed to turn our lights on and off and turn on the brighter multicolored lights that had been added to each aircraft. I really feel that the people who saw us from the ground could have mistaken us for a UFO. I know we are not responsible for all the reports since we only started flying after the sightings began in 1983. Also, I saw a UFO myself in 1982 . . . it wasn't any formation of planes I had ever seen!"

The caller gave me further information about certain CIA operations at Stewart and made me promise not to reveal the last bit of information, but I can tell you it had something to do with the Iran-Contra affair in 1986.[1] If there was

---

1 The Iran-Contra affair was a political scandal that came to light in November 1986 during the Reagan administration. Chief American military and political figures agreed to facilitate the sale of arms

indeed an alien-government connection involving the CIA, USDA, and military at Stewart Air Field, this would indicate that certain members of the United States government may have already had contact with the intelligence behind the Hudson Valley UFO.

Suspiciously, my informant mentioned a total of six planes, instructed to fly in those tight formations, but I remember viewing them in binoculars—there were eight. Since the total number of planes seen that night was not the same as what the informant told me, I began to question the validity of his call.

## Contact and Cover-Up

In response to what was taking place in the Hudson River Valley, I, along with UFO investigator Peter Gersten and writer Patrick Huyghe, organized a UFO conference with a public meeting format in Brewster, New York, in 1984. To our surprise, well over one thousand people attend the twelve-hour meeting, most of whom had sightings and were looking for answers. Gersten decided to create a new paranormal organization he called Contact. Contact's primary mission was to explore all claims of alien contacts with human beings. Peter invited some of the most well-known UFO researchers at the time to join the organization. Included in this elite group were Budd Hopkins and myself. For reasons I still do not understand to this day, Gersten dissolved the

---

to Iran to secure the release of hostages and fund the Nicaraguan contras.

organization shortly after it was formed. During our first and only meeting, members who had flown in from different parts of the country told tales of being followed by mysterious human agents, and one individual claimed agents had paid a visit to his home and told him the organization would never get much further than the planning stage. Well, this proved true because shortly after our first meeting, Gersten dissolved Contact.

Several months later, I received a call from a well-known Hollywood writer who said that a company called LBS Productions was putting together a live television special called *UFO Cover-Up: Live* wherein the government was going to release classified information about UFOs and alien contacts to the public for the first time. This person told me that Mike Farrell of the television show *M\*A\*S\*H* had agreed to host the show due to his great interest in the UFO phenomenon. I also found out that Mr. Farrell had read my book *Night Siege*, and thought that the sightings in the Hudson Valley were very important and should be included in the show. The writer, the producer, and some of the crew flew to New York City, where I met with them in the dining room of Mr. Farrell's hotel. My first impression was that this was just going to be another routine show about UFOs, but when they described the format, I got a very big surprise.

I was told the show would be live, and the government was going to allow the showing of alien contact that had taken place at Holloman Air Force Base in Alamogordo, New Mexico. Holloman Air Force Base is adjacent to White Sands National Monument in the Tularosa Basin, and is the home of the 49th Tactical Fighter Wing. On July 16, 1945, the first atomic bomb was detonated in the base's northwest corner and is known today as Trinity Site. Holloman has always been a high security area, so it's understandable why this location was chosen for the first alien contact. On May 23, 1971, two discs and one triangle-shaped craft appeared over Holloman AFB in the nearby desert.[2] A craft landed, and three humanoid occupants emerged and were greeted by scientists and military representatives. All or most of the landing episode is allegedly captured on several hundred feet of 16mm color film.

Representatives of military intelligence agreed to appear on the show and announce that UFOs are real, and that an alien intelligence had been visiting our planet for a very long time. I was told that they considered my part in the program very important, and they hoped I would travel to Washington when the air date arrived. I was asked not to talk about the format of the show to anyone, but can you imagine how difficult it was to keep that kind of information quiet? How would any of my readers feel if they were just told that in the near future, there was going to be an announcement that UFOs are real and they are the product of an alien intelligence? This type of secret is almost impossible to keep. In the time that followed, I was quite excited about what was going to happen, but remained skeptical. It didn't really

---

2 This is the year given to me during the meeting, although if you look up the date of the landing online, you might get confused: dates for the alien-human meeting are given as 1955, 1964, and 1992. Perhaps more than one meeting took place, perhaps not.

make sense, why after all the years of cover up, the government was finally going to release this type of information to the public. If the military was going to announce that they had been in contact with an extraterrestrial intelligence, it would be like dropping a super-atomic bomb on the world, and the effects might be devastating. Such knowledge of an alien intelligence might have severe effects on our economy, science, and religion. Every aspect of our culture would be changed—some for the better, but perhaps some for the worse.

About a week later, a second meeting was scheduled in New York City, this time involving the producers and several UFO researchers who prefer to remain anonymous. Later, we were joined by two individuals dressed in black suits who only identified themselves as Mr. Smith and Mr. Jones. I asked boldly who they were and was told they worked for a very secret part of the government that would be supplying the information for the show. I questioned this, and one of them pulled out a folder saying it was my "jacket," a term used in the military and intelligence agencies as a personal folder. In this "jacket" was information about me, including schools I'd attended and my military record. Mr. Smith and Mr. Jones had everything on me![3] I was convinced beyond a doubt that they represented a very powerful military or paramilitary organization, and I took whatever they had to say very seriously. They went on to say that just before air time, they would supply the production

---

3 I kid you not—despite this taking place well before the MIB movies, both these men could have had starring roles!

with all the required documentation and a representative from their organization would announce live that what was about to be seen was not special effects, but an actual event that had taken place. It seemed unbelievable that our government was going to announce to the world—on live television—that it has been in contact with an alien intelligence for almost fifty years. As I sat there and listened to everyone talk, it almost felt dreamlike. After all, things like this don't happen in the real world . . . at least that's what I was brought up to believe! I thought to myself, "Any minute now, Phil, you're going to wake up." But this *wasn't* a dream—it was real and I was going to be part of the most important event in human history.

The show's air date drew closer, and I never got the phone call to travel to Washington. I found out later that whoever the two government men were and whatever organization they represented had backed out at the last moment; they were not going to turn over the Holloman film to the producers. As a result of this, the staff at the production company had to rewrite the entire format of the show on a moment's notice. When *UFO Cover-up: Live* finally aired, it came across as so disorganized and ridiculous that the show actually hurt the study of UFOs rather than help it. I am not sure what really took place, but it had something to do with a well-known UFO-paranormal writer who was often accused of being a government informant (not me, for once!). Somehow, some way, this person stepped in at the last moment to rewrite the show's entire format. The new program centered on the testimony of one so-called government agent who remained in the shadows and discussed things like how the aliens enjoyed eating strawberry ice cream. This made many viewers laugh at the show, and in effect made the study of the phenomenon look downright silly. In the months to follow, the writer publicly admitted he was an informant for an unnamed intelligence organization in the government. Actor Mike Farrell was so discouraged by the program that he later announced that he would never do another television program again concerning the UFO phenomenon.

Perhaps our government planned to pull the plug all along: they promised the producers all kinds of earth-shattering information, then at the last moment, pulled the rug out from under the producers, making everything fall apart. However, there are some who believe they *did* plan to deliver the promised information, but at the last minute, there was disagreement in this secret organization and the "good guys" who wanted to work with the producers lost and disappeared. Whatever the reason, it made many people turn their backs and laugh at not only UFO witnesses, but UFO researchers as well.

Despite the negative impact of *UFO Cover-up: Live*, I still received quite a few credible reports, and by end of the year 2000, my files contained hundreds of unexplained cases. Since a great deal of my research had been published in various magazines, correspondence came in from all over the world. I received letters describing encounters not only with UFOs, but also with some unknown intelligence that seems to be connected to the phenomenon. The interesting thing about all these cases is that it didn't matter what part of the world they came from—the encounters were all the same. People all over our planet were experiencing the same thing! Most of these reports came from Europe, South America, the United States, Canada, Mexico, and Japan. I also received several dozen cases from Australia. Sometimes, I would get two or three letters from the same person, asking about their first letter and why there was no response. The truth of the matter is that in some cases, I never received a first letter! This led me to suspect that someone out there was intercepting my mail, but for what reason? My files have always been open to any qualified researcher, and most of my work has been published. If someone in the government was opening my mail, they'd be wasting their time—all they'd have to do is pick up a copy of a UFO-paranormal magazine or read one of my books.

### Air Force Assistance and Missing Mail

The number of letters that never arrived grew. Then, out of the blue and to my great surprise, I received a call from a representative from the air force. The caller identified himself as a Major Andrews and said he was calling from Burlington, Massachusetts. Major Andrews' official title was the Air Force Liaison to the FAA. This call was quite a surprise: here was a senior officer on the phone who wanted to discuss UFOs, a topic the air force considered taboo. The major wanted to know how many reports I had of sightings in the New York area. I told Major Andrews there were hundreds of reports given by sane, credible citizens and that I was convinced the things they saw were real, unknown objects, and not some type of elaborate hoax. The major replied by saying that the air force was very concerned about the UFO sightings in the New York area, although some of the reports could be attributed to a secret surveillance device that has been tested at high altitudes over the East Coast. The Major seemed only interested in gathering information, and at times, it seemed as if he was reading questions off some kind of form. There was no doubt in my mind that he was merely collecting information for a higher authority, and that he knew very little about the UFO phenomenon personally.

Every time I tried to change the subject, the major skillfully redirected the conversation back to questions about UFOs. He was very interested in the sightings that took place over the Indian Point nuclear reactor in 1984 (mentioned in the first chapter of this book). He told me the air force was very concerned about the increase of sightings in the area and that they didn't want a "UFO scare on their hands." He also said that the air force was investigating the sightings, and asked if I would cooperate in exchange for information. I agreed to cooperate as much as possible, providing the air force send me sighting reports that they recently obtained in the tri-state area. Once again, the major agreed, but I was a little suspicious—the air force officer seemed almost *too* eager to cooperate. The conversation lasted about forty-five minutes and ended with the major promising to send me a number of reports and documents that might aid me in my research. The conversation ended on a positive note and at no time was there any pressure or threat of any kind. The major just seemed to be doing his job and when he felt he got all the information he needed, he ended the call.

Several weeks later, I received a packet in the mail from the Air Force Intelligence sector in Washington, DC, containing a number of reports. Although most of the documents didn't contain any earth-shattering information, there were a few interesting ones. There were several reports from FAA air traffic control operators at the Islip, Long Island, tracking station reporting unknown targets on their screens. They asked the air force what they should do about UFO reports from private and commercial pilots. There was also an original letter—not a copy—addressed to well-known UFO investigator and dear friend the late Bob Pratt from a woman in Tennessee. The letter described a close encounter she'd had with a triangle-shaped UFO. This sighting was also witnessed by local law enforcement, the military, and at least ten other people. I called Bob and described the letter to him. He told me that he never received it, but knew about the sighting; he had written a story about it. How did this letter end up in the hands of the air force, and why give it to me, knowing that Bob and I had worked together in the past? If we assume the letter was placed in the documents by mistake, then the only possible answer is that I was never meant to receive it. This just about proved once and for all that someone in the government was not only intercepting some of my mail, but possibly that of other well-known UFO investigators as well.

## The Mountain City UFO

In 1994, I received a call from an excited person named Steve Smith from Mountain City, Tennessee. After reporting a UFO to the air force by phone, Steve was accidently connected to some type of secret military operation whose main purpose seemed to be recovering alien technology.

What started as an average evening at home with his family had turned into the starting point of an adventure he may not have wanted to partake in. On the evening of November 15, 1994, at 7:10 PM, Steve was at home playing a computer game. Hearing a helicopter outside, he went out to investigate, this being the fifth one of the day. All Steve could see was a blue strobe light flashing, but as he turned to go back inside, something caught his eye. Steve was amazed to see a huge craft fly over the hill with eleven lights glowing on the bottom and two small lights on the front. He described the movement of the object as drifting rather than flying. He ran into the house to tell his family, and they all came outside to see the strange object. They were able to watch it for about fifteen minutes. The object looked saucer-shaped, but they couldn't make out a distinct geometric outline. The only sound that came from the object was that of air rushing over it as it moved. The UFO flashed its lights at Steve and his family and moved away. The rest of the evening was uneventful and the Smith family settled down to watch some TV. At about ten o'clock, they all retired to bed for a good night's sleep. At four in the morning, Steve's wife and daughter woke from sleep apparently very ill—a trip to the emergency room seemed to be the appropriate action to take. It was discovered that his wife and daughter had very high fevers. After several hours and the proper medication and fluids, their body temperatures returned to normal and they were allowed to go home with follow-up instructions to see their doctor the next day. The cause of the fevers was never discovered. In my files are eight similar cases where people became ill after a UFO passed close by them. Why Steve did not become ill is not known for sure, but UFOs are known to emit certain types of radiation that could compromise the human immune system. At this time, I don't have absolute proof to support my theory, but radiation exposure and/or poisoning is something UFO investigators must consider.

Over the course of the following week, Steve felt strongly that he should report the sighting of the UFO to someone in the government, in hopes of getting some answers as to what he saw that night with his family. The local and state police were of no help; when he called the local radio stations and newspapers, they seemed uninterested in hearing "flying saucer stories." After waiting about a month, he finally worked up the nerve to report what he had seen to the air force. He called the 1-800 number and was given the number of Patrick Air Force Base in Florida where an on-duty officer answered and took his report.[4] He was then transferred to a Colonel Wilson, who told Steve that he was

---

4 Patrick AFB is home to the 45th Space Wing and controls all launches of unmanned rockets at Cape Canaveral Air Force Station. These rockets include satellites for the military and National Security Agency. It's possible that any type of foreign or unknown technology may be handled from this location.

a social psychologist. He started asking Steve questions about his encounter as if he was reading from a UFO "questionnaire form." He wanted to fly Steve down to Florida to make a statement. Steve had to decline, since he was unable to travel because of job demands. Steve asked the colonel if he knew what the object was that he had seen. The colonel replied, "We know that they are unidentified, but we don't know if they're extraterrestrial or where they come from."

The colonel then transferred Steve to a major who said he was an audiologist. He could barely hear the major because there was a very loud radio in the background. The radio contact sounded like communication between two fighter pilots. Steve could clearly hear them say: "Eagle has UFO on screen . . . will disperse now. Struck! The Eagle has struck!" Steve thought the major put his hand over the phone, because he heard him in a muffled voice yell, "Someone get that radio and silence it through security mode, I've got a (some kind of code word or name for Steve) on the telephone!" Then he heard one of the pilots over the radio say, "It's on the ground . . . Professor, you've got to get down here now to—" The major cut him off and yelled, "That can't be disclosed!" He got back on the phone with Steve and said, "Sorry there's so much noise here. I've got to go." He took Steve's telephone number and said he would call him back. The next day Steve called the exact same number and got the helicopter rescue unit on the airfield instead. This time, a woman answered and she said she didn't know any Colonel Wilson or the major Steve was trying to reach.

## *My Attempt*

Steve gave me the number, so the next day, I called and got the same results. Two days after that, I called again to try and get information but the number had been disconnected. I tried the number again two weeks after that, and was greeted by a recording that said "All classified calls are now being directed to Andrews Air Force Base. Before we transfer your call, please have your name, phone number, and social security number ready to give the operator." At first I hung up, but later called back and gave the operator the required information. I was surprised when another operator answered, stating she was the public information officer at the Pentagon. When I asked about UFOs in the Tennessee area and Steve's phone call, I was told, "The military does not investigate UFOs since it was found they posed no threat to national security." I was also told that if I would like a copy of the report, the Pentagon would gladly mail the final findings of the study done by Dr. Edward Condon.[5] I declined, politely thanked the operator for her cooperation, and hung up. Thinking about it afterwards, the entire matter seemed very fishy to me—like further evidence of a government cover-up.

---

5  This refers to a 1968 report called "Scientific Study of Unidentified Flying Objects" by Dr. Edward Condon of Colorado University. In it, after studying fifty-six UFO cases, Dr. Condon recommended the air force cease investigations of UFOs because they offered no scientific information. (Condon, Edward U. "Scientific Study of Unidentified Flying Objects." Springfield, VA: National Technical Information Service, 1968. Reprint, New York: E. P. Dutton, 1970.)

---

Since Steve's initial sighting in November, the object has been sighted by a growing number of people in the Mountain City area. The strange object can be seen gliding across the mountains and dipping into the valley almost every clear night. Being quite tenacious, Steve has done a great deal of follow-up, asking people in the area if they have seen anything strange. A couple owning a small cafe on a hilltop spent the summer watching the object at least twice a week as it glided over the area very low in the sky. Another man admitted to having seen the object (or something similar) as far back as three years before Steve's sighting. More recently, the UFO has been seen flying even lower in the sky accompanied by two other objects. Steve and a number of witnesses finally got a look at the true shape of two of the objects as they crossed the disc of the full moon. All witnesses reported a definite geometric shape described as an equilateral triangle. Although the third object didn't cross the moon, it looked circular and was much smaller than the other two.

By late December, WCYB, a television station in Bristol, Virginia, had mentioned the UFO sightings quite frequently. One evening, right before the weather report, the meteorologist said there had been a sighting, and anyone with a camera who could get it on video would have the pleasure of seeing it on the air the next night. Steve went out to look for it. He was able to see it once again moving over the mountains but unfortunately didn't own a video camera. Someone else did, however, and the UFO was shown on the local news the next night, as promised. I was able to see the video, but it was of low quality with a great deal of shaking. It showed two sets of lights in a triangular formation moving slowly, at a considerable distance from the camera.

During and after the UFO sightings, residents reported numerous unmarked black helicopters flying at a low altitude. Only a few departments in the government are allowed to fly without any markings; they include the CIA, NSA, and NSC. Steve really wished he had never seen this unexplainable object—he finds himself plagued with the desire to know what the object is, where it came from, and most importantly, what was it doing so close to his home.

One would think that with all this activity, the Tri-Cities International Airport (in nearby Blountville) would have received reports of UFOs and tracked something on radar. It was a lead that was worth a shot, so on January 9, 1995, I called the airport and spoke with the assistant supervisor at the control tower. He asked me to call back in four hours so he could review any past logs. When I called back, he was "not available," so the secretary took my number. The assistant supervisor never called back. I tried several more times over the next week but was always told he was out or at a meeting. In February, I decided to write a letter to the airport supervisor asking about UFO reports from August to January of 1994 and 1995. Three weeks later, I received a handwritten note on airport stationery: "Nope, don't got any of those. Sorry."

## Conflict Over the Bering Strait

If you are a UFO investigator and are lucky enough to receive a considerable amount of media exposure, sooner or later you'll be contacted by someone who claims to have been a former military member who has "important information concerning the government's involvement with UFOs." Since 1980, I have been approached by five people with such a claim, and although all of them have unverifiable stories, they are all very interesting. It must be noted that these people have nothing to gain by reporting experiences they had while in the military, and none of them wanted any type of publicity. In the majority of these cases, the individual keeps the information secret until he or she feels enough time has passed to safely talk about it. Out of the five cases that came to my attention from 1984 to 2009, only one person presented documentation and credentials proving that he was at one time a high-ranking officer in the air force. This case is presented below. Although the story was told to me fifteen years ago, this is the first time it is being published.

In 1994, I was approached by a person who claimed to be a retired Air Force lieutenant colonel whose last assignment was a Deputy Wing Commander for the 3rd Fighter Wing at Elmendorf Air Force Base in Alaska. If the story he told me that day is true, it could be considered verification that a covert section of the military was or is still trying to capture UFO technology. The individual was in his late sixties and identified himself only as "Starbuck." Although I met this person in an isolated part of Putnam Valley, he would not allow any pictures or audio recordings of him or his statement.

Starbuck says it all began with sightings of unidentified objects coming from Siberia over the Bering Strait in March of 1990. They were first picked up by Eielson Air Force Base.[6] The commander of that base called the control room at Elmendorf to scramble two F-15 Eagles in an attempt to identify the unknown targets. Starbuck was on duty that day, and when the call came in, he notified his commander to report to the control room. The commander ordered two F-15 Eagles to deploy and get a positive identification on the "bogeys." As the F-15s approached, they acquired visual contact and reported three dark triangle-shaped aircraft at 23,000 feet moving in an easterly direction at 542 mph. As the jets approached, the objects seemed to gain altitude. The pilots were commanded to lock their Sidewinder missiles on one object; as they did, the electrical systems of both jets failed. Then without warning, the mysterious aircraft vanished without a trace. The pilots regained control of their aircraft and were ordered to head back to base. The commander then called the Pentagon to inform his supervisor of what had happened and was instructed that the next time the bogeys appeared, he had clearance to fire on them and bring them down. Eighteen hours later, two objects appeared on the radar screen. The commander scrambled two F-15 Eagles to intercept. This time, the pilots came within

---

6 Eielson AFB, Alaska, is located about twenty-five miles southeast of Fairbanks, and is the home to the 354th Fighter Wing, assigned to the 11th Air Force in the major command of the Pacific Air Forces. The 354th FW supports operations, maintenance, mission support, and medical functions in the Pacific, and is host to ten tenant units including Alaska's Air National Guard 168th Air Refueling Wing.

firing range; both locked on one of the targets. As they were about to fire their missiles, both aircraft lost power and fell into the sea. The UFOs then vanished on radar and weren't seen again that day. Starbuck was very certain that both aircraft and their pilots were lost. A rescue mission later would find the aircraft in the sea, but the men were missing.

Almost exactly twenty-four hours after the second failed reconnaissance attempt, one unknown object was picked up in the same position over the Bering Sea. The commander notified the Pentagon and was instructed to intercept and bring down the unknown craft using any means possible. The commander told the general at the Pentagon, "No sir, I will not send any more aircraft until you tell me what we're dealing with. I won't lose any more aircraft or people." Both the commander and Starbuck argued with the general on the other end of the line; both refused to obey his order. The next day, the commander of the base was relieved of duty and was forced to resign his commission. Starbuck and another major were the second and third officers in the control room at the time, and within one week of the incidents, they were both given early retirements. In a debriefing, they were told that the incidents were classified as top-secret, and any discussion about what took place would result in prosecution. Starbuck concluded by saying, "I haven't talked about this in years. My friend, the major, moved to a cabin in Vermont. One day, he went to the press with the story about the UFOs and our loss of the F-15s and pilots. The story was never published, and five days later, he vanished off the face of the Earth. They found his cabin empty with no sign of struggle. His family thinks he went fishing one day and drowned in the lake, but his boat was still tied to the dock. A body was never found."

F-15 fighter jets are quite expensive, so one would think that when two aircraft are lost, someone would know about it and the event would be recorded, as Congress is notified of all military losses. An investigation on my part revealed that in March of 1990, an F-15 from Elmendorf was damaged in an operation over the Bering Sea.[7] The official explanation was that another F-15 pilot accidently fired his Sidewinder missile at the jet, causing damage to the aircraft. The news story goes on to say that the pilot didn't die in the accident, but it isn't clear whether he was able to land the jet or if he ejected to safety.

## The MJ-12 Controversy

In the mid-eighties, a number of documents started circulating within the civilian UFO community that caused quite a sensation. These documents, known as the "Majestic 12" or "MJ-12," told of a top-secret committee within the United States government organized shortly after World War II to study alien beings and their craft. When I received my own copies of the documents and read them, it was exciting at first, but then it struck me as too good to be true. I know for a fact that our secretive government doesn't allow information like this to leak, especially documents dubbed "Classi-

---

7 "Jet Pilot Accidentally Fired Live Missile, Air Force Says." *New York Times*, June 28, 1990.

fied" and "Top Secret." They're also not likely to be mailed in brown envelopes to people involved with UFO investigations. Well, that's precisely how the person who began circulating them claimed they came into his possession.

After twenty-five years of looking over the MJ-12 documents, most civilian investigators of the UFO phenomenon feel the documents are fakes. I won't get into the controversy surrounding MJ-12 in this book, but if you would like more information, a considerable amount of published material is available on the Internet. However, I must warn you that the majority of websites that have appeared over the past five years concerning MJ-12 are quite radical, filled with paranoid claims and government conspiracy theories. At this point in time, I feel the documents are indeed forged, a conclusion I base on my experience in the military, knowing the many checks and balances that take place in the handling of sensitive classified material, but it's just my opinion.

For those of you who do not know anything or little about the Majestic 12 documents, here's a brief history.

———

"Majestic 12" is the alleged code name of a secret committee of scientists, military leaders, and government officials formed in 1947 by an executive order from President Truman. The purpose of the committee was to investigate UFO activity in the aftermath of an alleged crash of an alien spacecraft near Roswell, New Mexico, in the summer of 1947. The primary evidence for the existence of a group named "Majestic 12" is a collection of documents that first emerged in

1984 which state: The Majestic 12 group was established by order of President Truman on September 24, 1947. The elite group of assorted specialists were given the task of dealing with an alien intelligence that was now in contact with the United States government."

In 1986, the FBI investigated the documents, and concluded they were forgeries, based primarily on an opinion rendered by the air force Office of Special Investigations. Opinions among UFO researchers are divided: some argue the documents may be genuine, while others contend they are phony, primarily due to errors in formatting and chronology.

In 1985, another document mentioning MJ-12 dated 1954 was found in a search at the National Archives. Its authenticity is also highly controversial and most feel the person doing the search planted the document to make it look like it was discovered. Since the "leak" of the first MJ-12 documents, hundreds of pages of additional supposedly leaked government documents mentioning MJ-12 and a government cover-up of UFOs have appeared on the Internet. After looking at them, it's quite easy to tell that they're fakes. With today's technology, it's quite easy to type up anything on the computer and paste it into a government agency's letterhead. When asked about all the alleged "secret government documents" that have appeared over the years, I simply reply, "I believe most of them are fake. Whatever we have in the form of documents is exactly what this secret agency in the government allows us to have." It's hard to believe that so many people are coming forward with so many secret documents that expose the government's involvement with UFOs. Recently, a new document appeared via the Internet that was classified as top-secret. It mentions a "Project Aquarius" and contact with aliens. The document was signed simply as "MJ3." I laughed when I read the "top secret" document—it was full of misspellings and grammatical errors my eighth grade class wouldn't make even on a bad day.

It's highly implausible that all these "MJ" people who in the past have been listed as coming from Ivy League schools would make such simple mistakes. Also adding to my doubt are the people in the UFO field who continually attempt to falsify information to get themselves on radio and television for a moment of fame. Well, I briefly touched on an issue of national security with the UFO sightings at the Indian Point nuclear plant and was swiftly reprimanded. That's another reason why I find the idea of documents mysteriously and conveniently "leaking" into the hands of UFO investigators difficult to accept.

### One Final Thought

I wasn't going to include the information below, but decided I should—it might shed some light on this entire MJ-12 controversy. In 1970, while serving in the military in southeast Asia, I was assigned to a unit that gave medical support to a number of operations in Thailand and Cambodia. One day, I was told to report to my commander, a full-bird colonel in the intelligence sector.[8] The colonel wasn't in, so I sat down

---

8  For those unfamiliar with military terminology, a "full-bird" colonel is a term (though not a proper direct address) for the full rank of colonel, as opposed to the lower-ranking lieutenant colonel. The "bird" refers to the eagle in this rank's insignia.

in his office and waited. Usually whenever I was called into his office, it meant some type of disciplinary action for me; I was always getting into trouble for not obeying orders.

I got up out of my chair and looked on his desk, hoping to see something that would indicate how much trouble I was in. On his desk was a document named "Project Majestic." I skimmed the document quickly and saw that it had something to do with the government and military taking control over the people of the United States in a time of emergency. It stated that the control would have to be willing (like making civilians think that turning to the military for protection was their own idea), and that fear should be induced within the American public so it would give total control over to the military for protection. The document brainstormed ideas that would induce the most fear in the general populace, including natural disasters, threats of World War III, virus outbreaks, terrorist attacks, and even the idea of an alien invasion. The document indicated that major members of the media would be included in this plan and it would be known as a "contingency plan for survival of the human race after WWIII and other threats." Is it remotely possible that someone may have seen this document, and from it got the idea that it would be a good name for a faked document we know today as "Majestic," or is it all just a coincidence?

# TWELVE

# AN ANALYSIS OF THE CONTACT EXPERIENCE

Recently, I had to take a large percentage of my older files and store them in my garage, in waterproof boxes. I'm running out of shelf room in my study; there are so many thick binders full of material. If there was a quicker way, I would put all the cases studies I've accumulated over the last thirty plus years and digitize them on CDs. It wasn't possible to present every contact experience I've investigated in this book, but an analysis of the numbers can be shown in charts and graphs to help the reader get a better understanding of this phenomenon as a whole.

## Chart 1: Site Condition from a
## Close Encounter of the Second Kind (CE-II)

A Close Encounter of the Second Kind is when the UFO leaves behind some kind of physical evidence. In the chart below, the object affected the ground in some way. Most of the data was obtained in the northeastern United States, but some of the events were reported to me from various parts of North America. This study is based on 221 cases from 1982 to 1998. I included this aspect of the UFO phenomenon because a CE-II can be considered the most distant type of contact case.

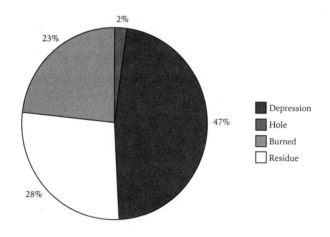

## Chart 2: Type of Beings Reported in Contact Cases

This chart has changed over the past ten years with reports of reptilian or insect-like beings becoming as numerous as the Grays. It must also be noted that the category of "Other" mostly consists of shadow-like beings, sometimes called "shadow people." This study is based on 259 cases from my files covering the time period of 1982 to 2009.

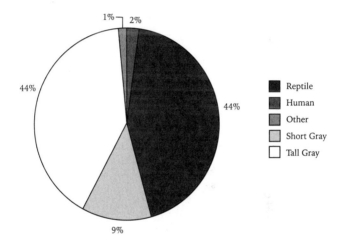

1%  2%

44%

44%

9%

Reptile
Human
Other
Short Gray
Tall Gray

## Chart 3: Abduction Cases: Male

Based on 115 cases from 1975 to 2009, 19 percent of abductees showed some psychic ability or had a psychic experience with a history of contact since childhood. No specific blood type was noted, unlike cases of female abduction.

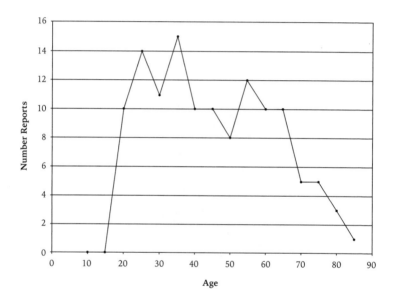

## Chart 4: Abduction Cases: Female

Based on 152 cases from 1976 to 2009, 83 percent had type B negative blood and 67 percent had psychic abilities or a past psychic experience. Ninety-two percent claim to have had an initial contact experience at a younger age. Eight percent had never had a previous UFO sighting.

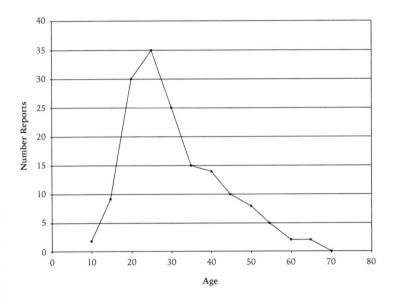

## Chart 5: Time of Contact Experiences

This chart is based on 137 cases from 1976 to 2008. Most of the experiences took place in the early hours of the morning while the person was in bed. In most cases, the person was paralyzed and the entity may or may not have communicated with him or her. In some cases, the person was taken out of the bedroom and transported to another place.

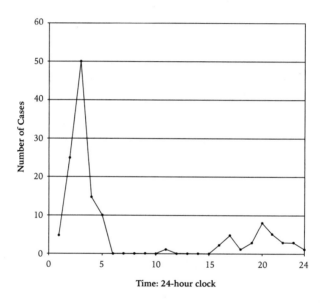

Time: 24-hour clock

## Conclusions

The contact phenomenon is very real. My investigations, in addition to the research being done by many others in the field, are uncovering which cases are increasing in frequency. At first, I thought the increase in reports was a result of people feeling more willing to talk about their experiences than in the past, but this may not be the case. The contact phenomenon affects people from all walks of life, from every culture around the world. No particular race, religion, or level of education is immune.

Some psychologists I have consulted with believe people who claim contact with an alien intelligence are actually looking for an escape from our troubled world. These experts consider it a psychosis of the twenty-first century, to put it bluntly. I disagree with their assertion; in a good number of cases I've investigated, the individual cared nothing about alien contact or UFOs prior to the contact or sighting. In some cases, the contact experience changed the subject's life so radically, they felt victimized. It seems illogical that an unhappy person would escape to a world that is worse. The real reason why the contact experience is increasing on a global scale is open for speculation, but let me remind you that speculation often leads to discovery. I'm continuing my exploration of this phenomenon, so if you've had an experience you would like to share, please contact me.

# A LIST OF UFO-PARANORMAL RESEARCHERS, GROUPS, AND PUBLICATIONS

**Philip Imbrogno**

pimbrogno@sbcglobal.net

bel1313@yahoo.com

Or write to me: c/o Llewellyn Worldwide

**New England Antiquities Research Association**

1199 Main Street

Worchester, MA 01603

Stone chamber research in New England.

**Paul Greco and Francine Vale**

**UFO Roundtable**

Yonkers Public Library (Will Branch Library)

1500 Central Park Ave

Yonkers, NY 10710

Meets on Wednesdays at 6 PM

uforoundtable@gmail.com

http://ufos.meetup.com/237/

### Another Reality Show

Hosted by Golden Hawk

goldenhawkfeather@yahoo.com

A great radio show about spiritual matters and the paranormal. Email Goldie for show dates and times.

### The Bigfoot Research Organization

http://www.bfro.net/

contact@bfro.net

Phone (949) 278-6403

Fax (949) 682-4809

Great database for you Bigfoot fans.

### Rosemary Ellen Guiley

Paranormal researcher/ author

http://www.visionaryliving.com/index.php

From Rosemary's site you can navigate to just about any place in the world of the paranormal!

### International Fortean Organization (INFO)

http://www.forteans.com/

PO Box 50088

Baltimore, MD 21211

## The Mutual UFO Network (MUFON)

http://www.mufon.com/
PO Box 369
Morrison, CO 80465-0369

## The Center for UFO Studies

http://www.cufos.org/
2457 W. Peterson Ave
Chicago, IL 60659

## Search Project for Aspects of Close Encounters (SPACE)

http://community-2.webtv.net/HEgeln/
SPACESearchProject/

## UFO Magazine

PO Box 1103
Marina Del Rey, CA 90295

## Intruders Foundation

http://www.intrudersfoundation.org/
PO Box 30233
New York, NY 10011

## Long Island Abductees' Support Network

Michelle Guerin
PO Box 383
Point Lookout, NY 11569

**Pennsylvania UFO Network (PUFON)**
156 Creekside Manor Drive
Lehighton, PA 18235

**Aerial Phenomena Research Organization (APRO)**
PO Box 51
Savanna, IL 61074

**National UFO Reporting Center**
http://www.nuforc.org/
PO Box 700
Davenport, WA 99122
Peter Davenport is the contact person

**Florida UFO Network**
P.O. Box 534
Havana, FL 32333-0534

# BIBLIOGRAPHY

The majority of the material used for this book was obtained from my files and current research. However, the publications listed here were used to check facts and provide additional information.

## Chapter One

Glazer, Paul. "Did Aliens Buzz Indian Point?" *Journal News*, October 22, 1984.

Hynek, Dr. J. Allen, Philip Imbrogno, and Bob Pratt. *Night Siege: The Hudson Valley UFO Sightings*. Woodbury, MN: Llewellyn Worldwide, 1998.

Maccabee, Bruce. "The McMinnville UFO." *News Register,* May 13, 2000.

Washington Correspondent. "Strange Objects in the Sky: Flying Saucers Seen on Radar Over Washington, DC." *New York Times*, July 22, 1952.

## Chapter Two

Dennet, Preston. *UFOs Over New York: A True History of Extraterrestrial Encounters in the Empire State.* Atglen, PA: Schiffer, 2008.

Smiley, James. "UFOs Seen Over Connecticut." *Hartford Courant,* March 27, 1997.

## Chapter Three

Hynek, J. Allen. *The UFO Experience.* New York: Ballantine Books, 1974.

Fagerstrom, Dean. *The Celestial Citizen.* Brewster, NY: Self-published, 1984.

Walker, Alan. *Franz Liszt, The Final Years: 1861–1866,* Volume 3. Ithaca, NY: Cornell University Press, 1997.

## Chapter Four

Hopkins, Budd. *Missing Time.* New York: Ballantine Books, 1988.

Irving, Washington. *Rip Van Winkle. Retold By Thomas Locker.* Golden, CO: Fulcrum Publishing, 2008.

## Chapter Six

Cana, Pronsias. *Celtic Religion: An Overview.* New York: Macmillan Reference, 2005.

The Holy Qur'an (Koran). Translated by Various. Noor Foundation International, 1977.

Kavanagh, Herminie. *Darby O'Gill and the Little People.* New York: Tor Fantasy Publishing, 2007.

Kirby, Paul. "A New York Bigfoot." *Kingston Freeman* (digital version) http:// www.dailyfreeman.com. July 10, 2008. Accessed July 11, 2008.

Levy, Joel. *Fabulous Creatures and Other Magical Beings.* London: Carroll and Brown Publishing, 2007.

Otfinoski, Steven. *Henry Hudson: In Search of the Northwest Passage.* New York: Benchmark Books, 2006.

Skinner, Charles. *Myths and Legends of Our Own Land.* Philadelphia: J. B. Lippincott Company, 1896.

Staff Writer. "Is the Catskills Home to Bigfoot?" *Catskill Digital Journal.* http://www.digital journal.com. Accessed July 12, 2008.

## Chapter Seven

Balzano, Christopher. *Ghosts of The Bridgewater Triangle.* Atglen, PA: Schiffer Publishing, 2008.

Putnam County Historical Society. *A Historical Account of Daniel Ninham.* Putnam County, NY, 1897.

## Chapter Ten

Marcel, Jesse and Linda Marcel. With Stanton Friedman. *The Roswell Legacy.* Pompton Plains, NJ: New Page Books, 2008.

Pazzaglini, Mario. *Symbolic Messages.* Trenton, NJ: Self-published, 1991.

Ruhlen, Merritt. *The Origin Of Language: Tracing the Evolution of the Mother Tongue.* Hoboken, NJ: Wiley Publishing, 1996.

Senner, Wayne. *The Origins of Writing.* Lincoln, NE: University Of Nebraska Press, 1991.

## Chapter Eleven

Author Unknown. Majestic Twelve ("MJ-12") documents.

Beckley, Timothy Green. *MJ-12 and the Riddle of Hangar 18.* New York: Inner Light-Global Communications, 1989.

Randle, Kevin D. *Case MJ-12: The True Story behind the Government's UFO Conspiracies.* New York: HarperTorch, 2002.

# RECOMMENDED READING

Dolan, Richard. *UFOs and the National Security State.* Newburyport, PA: Hampton Roads Publishing, 2002.

Friedman, Stanton. *Top Secret/Majic: Operation Majestic-12 and the United States Government's UFO Cover-up.* New York: Marlowe and Company, 1997.

Friedman, Stanton, and Kathleen Marden. *Captured! The Betty and Barney Hill UFO Experience.* Pompton Plains, NJ: New Page Books, 2007.

Guiley, Rosemary Ellen. *The Encyclopedia of Dreams.* New York: Berkley Publishing Group, 1995.

Hynek, Dr. J. Allen, Philip J. Imbrogno, and Bob Pratt. *Night Siege: The Hudson Valley UFO Sightings.* St. Paul, MN: Llewellyn Publishing, 1998.

Imbrogno, Philip J. *Interdimensional Universe: The New Science of UFOs, Paranormal Phenomena, and Otherdimensional Beings.* Woodbury, MN: Llewellyn Publishing, 2008.

Imbrogno, Philip J., and Marianne Horrigan. *Celtic Mysteries: Windows to Another Dimension in America's Northeast*. New York: Cosimo Publishing, 2005.

Marcel, Jessie, and Linda Marcel. *The Roswell Legacy: The Untold Story of the First Military Officer at the 1947 Crash*. Pompton Plain, NJ: New Page Books, 2008.

# INDEX

# GET MORE AT LLEWELLYN.COM

Visit us online to browse hundreds of our books and decks, plus sign up to receive our e-newsletters and exclusive online offers.

- **• Free tarot readings • Spell-a-Day • Moon phases**
- **• Recipes, spells, and tips • Blogs • Encyclopedia**
- **• Author interviews, articles, and upcoming events**

# GET SOCIAL WITH LLEWELLYN

www.Facebook.com/LlewellynBooks

**Follow us on**

www.Twitter.com/Llewellynbooks

# GET BOOKS AT LLEWELLYN

## LLEWELLYN ORDERING INFORMATION

## FILES FROM THE EDGE
*A Paranormal Investigator's Explorations into High Strangeness*
### PHILIP J. IMBROGNO

Ghost lights, otherworldly creatures, visits from another dimension. The most bizarre and amazing case studies from a renowned paranormal investigator are presented here.

In his thirty-year career, Philip J. Imbrogno has researched a vast array of fascinating supernatural phenomena—the perpetually haunted mines of Putnam County, New York; encounters with strange entities at sacred megalithic stones; Bigfoot, yeti, and other humanoids; sea creatures; psychic phenomena; the dangerous Jinn; and a vast array of life forms from other worlds. The author's objective, scientific analysis—combined with credible witness testimonials and Imbrogno's own thrilling experiences—provides eye-opening, convincing evidence of our multidimensional universe.

978-0-7387-1881-1
336 pp., 5 ³/₁₆ x 8          $17.95

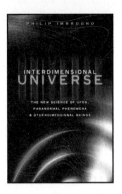

INTERDIMENSIONAL UNIVERSE
*The New Science of UFOs, Paranormal Phenomena*
*& Otherdimensional Beings*
PHILIP IMBROGNO

Over the course of his thirty years of investigation into UFOs, including his own field research, photographic evidence, and meticulously compiled case studies, Philip Imbrogno has provided fascinating new insight into paranormal phenomena. In this book, he reveals for the first time the detailed experiences of prominent paranormal experts as well as his own firsthand experiences. Using the latest quantum theories, Imbrogno sheds new light on classic UFO cases, government cover-ups, and the hidden connections between UFOs and other unexplained phenomena—from crop circles and animal mutilations to angels and jinns (or genies).

Imbrogno's intimate knowledge spans the very early UFO activities to present-day sightings. He personally investigated four of the best-known UFO flaps of the modern era—Hudson Valley, Phoenix lights, the Belgium sightings, and the Gulf Breeze, Florida sightings—and shares information never released before, including photographic evidence that something very unusual is taking place on planet Earth.

978-0-7387-1347-2
312 pp., 5 $^3/_{16}$ x 8          $17.95

## NIGHT SIEGE
### *The Hudson Valley UFO Sightings*
#### Dr. J. Allen Hynek, Philip J. Imbrogno & Bob Pratt

In 1983, just a few miles north of New York City, hundreds of suburbanites were startled to see something hovering in the sky. They described it as a series of flashing lights that formed a "V," as big as a football field, moving slowly and silently.

It has been seen many times since then, yet the media has remained silent about it, as have the military, the FAA, and the nation's scientists. Now, in *Night Siege*, expert UFO investigators reveal the amazing evidence that cannot be denied and the more than 7,000 sightings that cannot be dismissed.

A classic in the field, *Night Siege* has been called one of the best researched and factual UFO books to date. This second edition is revised and expanded with sightings up to 1995.

**978-1-56718-362-7**
**288 pp., 5³/₁₆ x 8**  **$9.95**

## ALIEN DAWN

*A Classic Investigation into the Contact Experience*

COLIN WILSON

In this classic book on UFOs, bestselling author Colin Wilson, a renowned authority on the paranormal, examines the evidence and develops a definitive theory of the alien contact phenomenon.

*Alien Dawn* covers Wilson's investigation into documented evidence of strange and unexplained phenomena, including UFOs, poltergeists, ancient folklore, time slips, out-of-body experiences, mystical awareness, and psychic travel to other worlds. The result: a fascinating and encyclopedic study of the complex nature of reality. This is one of the most comprehensive explorations of the subject undertaken, with conclusions sure to startle the reader, whether believer or skeptic.

**978-0-7387-1969-6**
**408 pp., 6 x 9**          **$18.95**

## MESSAGES

### *The World's Most Documented Extraterrestrial Contact Story*

STAN ROMANEK, WITH J. ALLAN DANELEK

We are not alone, and Stan Romanek can prove it.

From his first sighting of a UFO to chilling alien abductions, Romanek relives his personal journey as a conduit of extraterrestrial contact. But what's most shocking are the strange messages these unearthly visitors communicate to Romanek—authentic equations relating to space travel and planetary diagrams pinpointing what could be an auspicious date for the human race.

The national spotlight has followed Stan Romanek ever since the release of the "Peeping Tom" video of what he strongly attests is an actual extraterrestrial. Interviewed on *Larry King Live* and elsewhere, his true story of extraterrestrial contact is quite famous. More importantly, Romanek's gripping tale—augmented by video footage, photos, and physical evidence—is the most documented case of all time.

**978-0-7387-1526-1**
**288 pp., 6 x 9**          **$16.95**

## STRANGE BUT TRUE
### *From the Files of FATE magazine*
#### CORRINE KENNER & CRAIG MILLER

Have you had a mystical experience? You're not alone. For almost fifty years, *FATE* readers have been reporting their encounters with the strange and unknown. In this collection, you'll meet loved ones who return from beyond the grave, mysterious voices warning of danger, guardian angels, and miraculous healings by benevolent forces. Every report is a firsthand account, complete with full details and vivid descriptions:

978-1-56718-298-9
264 pp., 5³/₁₆ x 8          $12.95

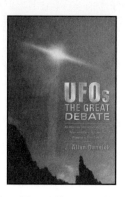

## UFOs: The Great Debate

*An Objective Look at Extraterrestrials, Government Cover-Ups, and the Prospect of First Contact*

J. Allan Danelek

Do UFOs really exist? Are we alone in the universe? Is the government hiding the truth from us? With his signature objective and balanced approach, J. Allan Danelek explores the controversial questions surrounding extraterrestrials that have raged for years.

This wide-ranging and captivating book begins with a historical overview of the decades-long debate, followed by an incisive look at the case for and against extraterrestrial intelligence. Danelek presents scientific evidence supporting UFOs and other life-sustaining planets, examines hoaxes, and raises practical objections based on radar findings and satellite observations. Next, he delves into government conspiracies and cover-ups—including Roswell, alien visitation, and alien technology. There's also intriguing speculation about the alien agenda—crop circles, alien abductions—and suggestions of possible scenarios, both benign and malevolent, for first contact with an alien race.

978-0-7387-1383-0
264 pp., 6 x 9     $15.95

## THE FOG

### *A Never Before Published Theory of the Bermuda Triangle Phenomenon*
### ROB MACGREGOR & BRUCE GERNON

Is there an explanation for the thousands of people who have disappeared in the Bermuda Triangle? What can we learn from Charles Lindbergh, Christopher Columbus, and Bruce Gernon—the coauthor of this book—who have survived their frightening encounters in this region?

*The Fog* presents Gernon's exciting new theory of the Bermuda Triangle, based upon his firsthand experiences, reports of other survivors, and scientific research. Gernon and MacGregor intelligently discuss how a meteorological phenomenon—electronic fog—may explain the bizarre occurrences in this region: equipment malfunctions, disorientation among pilots, and time distortions. They also explore the fascinating history of this infamous region and its potential link to Atlantis, UFO sightings, and a secret navy base on Andros Island.

Rob MacGregor has written several books on New Age topics and has won the Edgar Allan Poe award in mystery writing. Both Gernon and MacGregor live in South Florida, on the edge of the Bermuda Triangle. Bruce Gernon is a pilot who has flown extensively in the Caribbean. He has appeared in many documentaries about the Bermuda Triangle.

978-0-7387-0757-0
240 pp., 5 $^{3}$/16 x 8          $13.95

## UFOS OVER TOPANGA CANYON
### PRESTON DENNETT

The rural Californian community of Topanga Canyon is home to 8,000 close-knit residents, the Topanga State Park, and an unusual amount of strange activity going on in the sky.

Like Hudson Valley, New York, and Gulf Breeze, Florida, Topanga Canyon is considered a UFO hotspot, with sightings that began more than fifty years ago and continue to this day. Here is the first book to present the activity in the witnesses' own words.

Read cases of unexplained lights, metallic ships, beams of light, face-to-face alien encounters, UFO healings, strange animal sightings, animal mutilations, and evidence of a government cover-up. There are even six cases involving missing time abductions, and a possible onboard UFO experience.

**978-1-56718-221-7**
**312 pp., 5 $^3$/16 x 8**          **$12.95**

## To Write to the Author

If you wish to contact the author or would like more information about this book, please write to the author in care of Llewellyn Worldwide, and we will forward your request. Both the author and publisher appreciate hearing from you and learning of your enjoyment of this book and how it has helped you. Llewellyn Worldwide cannot guarantee that every letter written to the author can be answered, but all will be forwarded. Please write to:

Philip J. Imbrogno
$c/o$ Llewellyn Worldwide
2143 Wooddale Drive
Woodbury, MN 55125-2989

Please enclose a self-addressed stamped envelope for reply,
or $1.00 to cover costs. If outside the U.S.A., enclose
an international postal reply coupon.

Many of Llewellyn's authors have websites with additional information and resources. For more information, please visit our website at:

www.llewellyn.com